Just...Let It Be

To Sheila
You Pi Phi
Sister

Tricia

Also by Patricia Forbes

The Open Door: Meditations on Living an Authentic Life

Surfacing: A memoir

A Sign of His Love, a short story published in *Chicken Soup for the Couple's Soul*

Soul Mates, a short story published in *Chocolate for a Woman's Soul*

Just...Let It Be

Meditations on Living an Authentic Life

Patricia Forbes

Story Preserves, LLC
Denver, Colorado
www.storypreserves.com

Cover Photograph of Washington Park by Todd Egan

Interior Nature Photographs by Vince Hovley

Library of Congress Control Number: 2015941485

ISBN-13: 978-1-943324-00-2

ISBN-10: 194332400X

To my mother and father
who gave me life
and
to Richard Rohr
who changed my life

Acknowledgements

I give my deep gratitude to my spiritual teacher, Father Richard Rohr, a Franciscan priest who is a globally recognized Catholic and ecumenical Christian teacher. He is the founder and director of the Center for Action and Contemplation in Albuquerque, New Mexico. Father Richard, your messages strengthen my belief. They have taught me how to listen to my heart. Your words echo deep within and have opened me to more of the blessings of faith.

I also offer gratitude to Father Vince Hovley of Sacred Heart Retreat House in Sedalia, Colorado, for your inspirational and beautiful photography of nature.

And to Todd Egan, for the use of your photograph of Washington Park on the cover, I thank you.

Contents

Preface

Standing in the River of Life

Life is always a mixture, presenting different challenges and changes with each decade. Many of us would give anything to have a guidance book which covers all occasions but alas, we are left to find our individual way through pain and joy.

When I was presented with the demise of my mother, my husband, and two children within the space of 6 years it felt like being slammed into the hard cement of reality over and over again. I believe God grants the grieving a space of time in which the pain of loss is muted and numbed. Gradually, with help and my cooperation, in time the sad events opened wide the door of compassion, of deep understanding in me that wasn't identified before.

I knew I could not run away from the harsh reality, the closing of the "door of life" for family members who left too soon. It seemed that there was nothing else to lose, the bottom had dropped out of my world. And so, I gave myself over to feel their loss fully.

It was at these harsh times that I happened upon the teaching of Father Richard Rohr whose wise words poured restorative salve upon raw wounds and opened doors for me upon a new life, a deep spiritual essence that was inside me all the time.

The trick was not to close down but to keep an open heart in the in the midst of searing flames. These flames stripped away the debris of pettiness, of judgment, made clear the things that were important and the things that were not. A card by Teresa Savarin says "The greatest gift we can give those who have left us – is to live fully in their place." There followed a new view upon life for me.

And so, I write the following vignettes that might serve as a path through life's confusing brambles, hoping that you, my reader, might be thrown a life preserver of strength and hope.

WAKING UP

Life Quest

There are things
only you can do,
And you are alive
to do them.

In the great orchestra
we call life
You have an instrument
and a song.

Max Lucado

Looking at life through a wide lens now I see that it took many years to see the pattern - that I traveled in a rather tight group for a long time, like a stack of Indian dolls, each one removed revealing another identical doll. Whatever was the "norm," the community policy, what other people thought proper and right, I followed. I kept the status quo, walked in lock-step and was quite content.

There was also a lock-step in the family systems of the day, there's us and there is them. There seemed to be a lot of exclusion of anything or anyone else but our own.

Like a pair of shoes one has outgrown, I became aware that this structure was pinching me. It was constricting me. Like being in extremely high altitude, it became hard to breathe in the old system. Being raised in west Texas where one could look to the mountains on the horizon, my nature since childhood had been one of inclusion.

This elongated wide vision in which I still live in Denver, Colorado gives me a perspective on concerns and problems. It's a help in releasing the narrow, constant focus on me and mine.

In my early 40s during what might be best described as a midlife crisis, I began to plumb the depths of my inner self and understand in a new way how each human is given a gift and it is life's search to find that gift and use it for others as well as ourselves. Believing oneself in the company of only a selected few feeds the hungry ego that is always looking for more.

I love to write and teach. It's not only information that teachers transmit. Hopefully it's reaching the inner person, opening the "Ah-hah" moments for others, allowing the student to become the teacher.

I treasure my individuality and in my gift of continuing life I hope to hold onto and share a quiet peace that I am being graced with. I am ever grateful to finally recognize the joy of letting go into the hands of something undeniably loving that guides me. I call that something God.

River Lessons

Boulders stoically facing the rushing mountain waters
Refusing to move,
Hanging tenaciously and firmly
Onto life as it is.
Massive rock forcing the strident, tumbling energy
To part hands.

I wrote this poem while sitting on the bank of the river running through Vail. It reminded me of the amazing strength of the human spirit. The seemingly set-in-cement boulders have remained where they are forever, despite the fact that they are bombarded by the constant force of the river. As are human beings bombarded with life.

Daily we go unsuspecting through life. Rarely do I think about my fragility until some quick event strips life away from an acquaintance or loved one. An instant impulse can change the course of so many lives. Accidents happen that seem totally avoidable, some small slip that can change or erase the life of many.

I've watched people go through traumas that remind me of those stoic boulders. Things I myself do not think possible to survive. And yet, horrendous events did occur in my life and somehow I became one of those immovable boulders, refusing to be erased or step aside.

Certain statements like, "Bring it on!" probably was meant to indicate bravery. Not to me. That statement, if I were inclined to utter it, would bring about a quick, "Wait! I didn't mean that," directed to God above.

There is a time to step forward with strength, and a time to step back, with humility. Deciding which is which is the trick.

Timing is everything. Things I make room for today did not exist on a to-do list in my early years. Things relegated to the bottom of the list, today are prominent. At this stage of my life I begin my days with a quiet period asking my higher power to guide, direct, and lead my thoughts, actions, and especially my words, to put those people before me to whom I might be of service. When I stay alert to possibilities, it's amazing what and who appears.

To simplify: Any day to get out of myself is a good day.

Just...Be

Be present, be calm, be silent. My basic "Let me rescue you" self doesn't like this directive. It wants its old pattern: jumping in to change, fix, control things. Finally, I recognized the ego part of this equation. It is important to be aware of the "me" part of this urgent need to step in.

Until I suffered stunning, sudden losses my sneaky ego remained disguised on its throne. It seems that "I'm different, special and unique" lurks in most of us until some kind of inner fracture shatters this false image. I'm thankful for that day.

It can be something simple or it can be an earth shaking event that wipes out old beliefs.

Twelve Step Programs know this well. It's the basis for all of the steps, letting go of our old ways. Stale thoughts, like a worm digging down, keep sinking deeper in the unconscious and they exist until we wake up and become aware of them. I've been aware of this premise since middle age. But until events took me to my knees I couldn't let go of the belief I could change things and help avert pain for myself and others.

Growing up I noticed that everything rolled with a lot of effort, and just sitting, being, carried the unspoken translation of laziness. One must be productive. Until far into my adult years I felt I had to be sick, on an airplane, or going to sleep at night to feel okay about reading a book. Somehow it was not okay to just "be."

From personal experience I learned how to be of help to a grieving person. There are no words or busyness that comfort like your presence. Taking their hand in yours or not, offering no advice, asking no questions. Just being with that person with a loving heart is the comfort.

It's such a freedom to let go of the need to say something, filling the empty air. I like the thought that I tell myself when visiting adult children: Unless asked, nothing is required of you at this time. Although I like the thought, I'm sorry to say that I forget to practice it.

More often than not if only I pause and hold the tension, things resolve, as they were going to do anyway, no matter my involvement.

Buoyancy

I remember how exciting it was when my family took us to California every summer.

We land-locked souls from the desert of west Texas, reveled at just the sight of the grand ocean. As children, my brother and I ran into the waves shouting and laughing.

I can remember also the "amazing grace" of being automatically lifted into each swell.

Unlike the swimming pool at home, we didn't have to fight to stay above the water here in the ocean.

In Rumi's Poem, "Buoyancy" the last lines say:

So the sea-journey goes on, and who knows where!
Just to be held by the ocean is the best luck
We could have. It's a total waking up!
Why should we grieve that we've been sleeping?
It doesn't matter how long we've been unconscious.
We're groggy, but let the guilt go.
Feel the motions of tenderness
Around you, the buoyancy.

I recognize that my waking up came after the painful experiences of loss.

I can't say that the experience of buoyancy in my life continued uninterrupted. It was more like I quit fighting the current of life and just went with it. Often I call to mind that childhood joy, complete abandonment of fear as the ocean waters gently lifted me with no prompting. I realize today that I don't have to be in control. I can let go. With zero judgment, life's events are approaching in the ocean's next swell. All I have to do is go with it as gracefully as I am able.

Waking Up

"Who can open the door who does not reach for the latch" is a line in Mary Oliver's poem, *Have You Ever Tried to Enter the Long Black Branches?*

How that particular line grabbed my attention. I saw how long it had taken for me to be aware of my own self-absorption and step out into the busy world of otherness, of the simple joys of nature.

Richard Rohr states that about 90 percent of our thoughts are repetitive and useless, exploring the past and its regrets, or fears of the future. While few of us can stay in the moment, it is the goal. That is why falling in love is such joy. In the presence of the loved one, everything outside of pure presence fades into non-existence. This ideal time may not last but while it does, it opens the door to the precious now, which is all we have.

It's fun to be receiving validation for my childhood longing for something deeper, something not found in the visual world. As I wake up more and more, as I explore the beliefs of other spirits, the door to joy opens wider. I find that a small period of quiet every morning renews my desire to connect with the real, the authentic that surrounds us. This period of peace renews my awareness of the preciousness of right now and the desire to be open to whatever appears in my day. To be open to things other than pre-planned activities and duties. To go outside, observe trees that are coated democratically with fresh snow, see the crocus poking their heads up out of the soil, to wake up with a smile instead of dread.

On the afternoon side of my life-mountain now I want to continue to actively participate in the world. Being an introvert, it would be easy for me to retire from the world but I do myself and others a favor by just showing up and being with. That's all. No biggie. I carry a bundle of experiences, strength and hope which blooms the more it's shared.

We Are Not the Stories We Tell Ourselves

Clinical psychologist and meditation teacher, James Finley, tells us, in one of his talks that we are not who we think we are. We are not the situation we find ourselves in at the present moment. Nor are we our affliction. That's not our true self. The identity-images that we project are based on the stories we tell ourselves about ourselves. Along with Richard Rohr, Finley believes most of us share the human temptation to promote self-congratulatory presentations of ourselves. This is not a bad self doing this, it's just not our true self. It's the self we want the world to believe. The script has usually been formed in early childhood and followed our entire life, unless something disrupts the flow. That something is usually a disappointment or humiliation of some kind which throws the switch off. Then, an awakening to our authentic self has the opportunity to surface. We let change broaden us or we cling to the old pattern.

Growing older has a surprise in store. Midlife and beyond can be an illuminating time. As James Finley says, "no longer climbing upward, life can turn downward and inward into unbelievable richness." The fortunate ones who have done this can best be observed by the way they lead their lives: there is a vitality, a sense of balance about them. They seem to have a curiosity and a sense of awe about the people and the world in which they live.

In today's world of technology we're bombarded with pictures and words of who we should be, what lotion we should use, what profession we should be in, on and on.

It occurred to me even in my teen years how everything seemed to be judged on the outside, how it looked to others. My mother's leather bound classic books were not to be read necessarily, but admired on the shelf interspersed with plants.

Introversion seems to have come into sharper focus these days. Far from being left behind or finding themselves invisible to most of the world, introverts are now being recognized to a higher degree for the inner contributions that they make to others and the world. We find distinguished writers, poets, creative artists of all kinds to be the deep well of calm so needed in today's invasive overload of instant facts and information. The touchstone of spirituality flourishes in quiet landscapes. I believe we desperately need this interruption.

It Is What It Is

"What "should be" does not exist. What is, does."

So said Richard Rohr in one of his talks. Such wisdom lies in the simple acceptance of this fact. Let things be as they are. Respond, instead of react. Who, me? my mind counters.

In the poem "The Mind of Absolute Trust" by Seng- Ts'an, he says:

The Great Way isn't difficult
for those who are unattached to their preferences.
Let go of longing and aversion,
and everything will be perfectly clear.
When you cling to a hairbreadth of distinction,
heaven and earth are set apart.
If you want to realize the truth,
don't be for or against.
The struggle between good and evil
is the primal disease of the mind.
Not grasping the deeper meaning,
you just trouble your mind's serenity.
Because you select and reject,
you can't perceive its true nature.
Don't get entangled in the world,
don't lose yourself in emptiness.

Be at peace in the oneness of things
and all errors will disappear by themselves.
Step aside from all thinking,
and there is nowhere you can't go.
Don't keep searching for the truth;
just let go of your opinions.

What is wonderful about this wisdom poem is that you don't have to be a Buddhist or a Taoist, or anything else to intuit the truth of it. Most of us think that we are our thoughts. That's who we are. I believe that this poem represents the secret, the letting go of old, no longer useful ideas. I do this best by meditation, trying to empty the mind of relentless thoughts that carve the same old hurts and messages in the brain. To be able to do this is living in the now.

Roger Housden's comments about this poem states that if you loosen your attachment to a preference, then that, in itself, already opens up a larger space in consciousness. I believe that stepping back and being able to look with fresh eyes at a situation is the gift of such a practice. I can't do this with any kind of regularity, still I strive to do so.

Spoiled Child

Psychologist James Finley in one of his CDs said, "The mind is like a spoiled child. It goes where it wants to go, stays as long as it wants, says what it wants to say, does what it wants to do, with little correction." We just let 'er rip, don't we?

Thing is, I believe what my mind is telling me. I really think it's the truth. It bears exceptional fruit. At times I find myself pursuing some idiotic idea, "If only they knew what I know, things would be so much better." My spoiled child of a mind doesn't take stock of the facts of reality, it's not capable of doing this objectively. And it doesn't like contrasting ideas. Any idea contrary to mine is simply challenged. The child mind makes no room for reaching consensus, finding the middle of the ground.

That's how it used to be. But for me things are different now. What caused the break with the usual pattern? Pain in life happened. Tragedy enveloped me for most of the 1990s with the loss of family members. Finally, my lack of power was unveiled in its entirety. Ego, no longer the driver, reluctantly was forced to take a back seat.

I can more freely say, "I don't know" because I don't.

Now I can better recognize and spot the inconsistencies in my thinking. I pick up on my human traits better, and forgive myself, which is crucial. My new watchdog shakes it head and challenges self-pity parties, envy bouts, resentment parades. When all else fails, it turns to the one and only loyal entity that is always with me, that always reveals and protects me in everything from silliness, stupidity, ignorance of truth, and from my bumbling self. That entity is the God of my understanding. It is a deep inner "experience-with" type of knowing. And therefore it is extremely difficult, if not impossible to express in words.

But the total support is there. That's the point. My spoiled child bows its arrogant head to such a power. Thank you!

Beyond Right and Wrong

Beyond right and wrong, there is a field.
I will meet you there.

Rumi

Spiritual guides tell us that an adjustment in consciousness is needed in the second half of life. We need to develop a manner of being in the world that is broader, more expansive and inclusive if we are to continue growing. That level of consciousness contains the concept that nothing is all good or all bad. Everything is always a mixture.

Human nature seems to fall easily into the old black or white, up or down thinking. With this mind, as soon as something is before the brain, it is separated. One side we agree with, the other side must be wrong. We all started with this basic consciousness, using mainly our factual, left brain strength.

Two thousand years of schooling in right/wrong; good/bad vertical thinking did not encourage dwelling on spiritual philosophy. But in the enlargement of consciousness, there is no formal instruction, no memorization of texts, no strict adherence to dogma or code. This teaching is internal, experiential.

Wise teachers tell us that we don't throw anything away. We just add to it. We need both. We need the factual side of our brain, otherwise we wouldn't know how to get to our job, do our job, or other concrete necessities. The artist, the poet's right brain brings the imagination and balance.

The Oriental perspective looks beyond the mind altogether. It implies there is a wisdom already at work, the design which we can never really know. Or as Sufi poet Hafiz said, "There are plays within plays that you cannot see."

I don't think I would have given these thoughts any validity until I was forced by painful events to halt my "do it as usual" thinking patterns. Somehow there was relief in the "not knowing." Trusting this "not knowing" isn't a condition of laziness, of not caring. My ego forced aside, it became much easier to turn my life and will over to God. It became delight and wonderment that pushed me trusting into the unknown. Today, I find curiosity, not dread, in how each day unfolds.

It seems my mind is more spacious now. I can see adding different furniture and a variety of people!

Fly Paper

Fly paper traps annoying flies. They buzz around disturbing our peace, but if they light even momentarily on fly paper, they're captured. Whatever comes in contact with this adhesive tape is a graveyard for flying species.

I've found my brain at times acts like fly paper. Worry thoughts seems to get stuck there. Consciously trying to disengage my mind from a particular worry is like trying to extract a fly from restraining paper designed to hold it fast.

From where did this silly habit originate? I remember a childhood observation of the tiny lines that creased my mother's brow. I would ask, "Mom, what's the matter?" only to have her reply, "Oh, nothing. I just worry a lot."

I noticed that my mother worried most about family members, people she loved. Conversations about weather, the shopping center going up, or the mountain coyote that wandered down from the mountains into someone's back yard seemed not to produce the frown. But with talk about the problems of other family members, the worried brow would magically appear. So, in my childhood logic I connected the idea that worry equals love. If you love someone enough, the exhibited frowning brow was good.

This childhood belief set itself up comfortably in my head. Each time I run a worry or problem over again, it makes the groove a little deeper. To take charge of this annoying habit, I first become aware of its presence. "O.K.," I sternly tell the problem. "I'm going to let you in my head rent free. Spread out. Make yourself at home, but only for ten minutes!" Giving myself this time table, I concentrate hard on worrying – every possible scenario is gone over thoroughly. Then I dismiss, "Thank you for your concern and goodbye."

It works. But the lease and the threat of eviction unfortunately must be renewed again in the days to follow.

Something More

In Mary Oliver's beautiful poem *Have You Ever Tried to Enter the Long Black Branches?* she says, "Are you barely breathing and calling it a life?" What a powerful visual. It was many months after my husband died, I became aware of myself barely breathing while watching television one night. Since those dreary days I remind myself when tense to "just breathe" prompting me to take deep breaths.

As I advance in the ladder of years I recognize my childhood curiosity about everything continues as the years pass. I'm still in awe about life. For me, it's the study of how God operates in our lives and promotes compassion, love and forgiveness that grabs my attention. The most influential people in my life seem to have a degree in soulology.

But more than world knowledge, they come from a personal experience of God in their lives.

I picture a long hall in a house with many doors. Each one of us is born in this house. A large per cent of humans remain in this same area, choosing not to venture far. Some of us are lucky to leave this site and travel far and wide in the world. This opportunity is wonderful and broadening for anyone. But the concept that opens up the door of the soul I found is the inner adventure where a person dares to investigate the deeper part of themselves. Garrison Keillor said this at a graduation talk, "All that is essential is unseen." But most of us don't even desire to approach knowledge of the spirit until and unless we encounter failure in some way that steps on the outside image we've spent years building.

Sooner or later most of us come to a cross-roads where chance opens a path to go beyond our comfort zones, reach deep inside and risk knowing the truth about ourselves, to accept that we are all far from perfect. Then we begin to view with new awareness the situations in our lives. We can choose to seek something more. The fear of self-investigation binds many people with in-action. The deep secret I didn't know for so long is that unfortunately it is mainly through loss or failure, through disappointment or tragedy that this door unlocks. Very few who are swimming in beautiful surroundings and choose not to have a worry will even be tempted to question the soul's properties or even acknowledge its existence.

I am forever grateful that I discovered a pearl of joy residing in what appeared to be manure. I was willing to risk vulnerability, I kept going and I received what I wanted so badly – a connection with God and a new peace of mind, plus the desire to keep pursuing, keep learning.

Choice

It is said that there is a fine line between fear and excitement. Somehow I would never have thought to group those two words together. But that sentiment fits hopefully into a new pattern of living for me.

As life has continued to bombard us all with the good, bad, and ugly it has also continued to bombard us with gifts of love, bounty, and forgiveness. Recently I've come to another fork in my road. Again, instead of choosing the well-worn, busily traveled path of what looks like the most secure and same as usual, I now find myself open to the rocky, brambly path that was there all along.

Awareness of this other path is, for me at least, a strong indication of a shift in consciousness within. Instead of waking with expectations (and/or dread) of fulfilling what is on the calendar for the day, I wake up looking forward to who and what appears on the horizon. New possibilities are what I'm looking for now. New people, new conditions, new experiences.

I have always been acutely aware not only of the outer picture people present, but of my own and other's insides. This awareness has its price. But I'm finding that what I thought were filters against pain didn't work anyway. I try and dismiss the "judge" in me which wants to control. It's a whew! surrender mentally and emotionally. When drama appears on my horizon, a mantra I'm trying to establish internally says, "And then…" It's an effort to neutralize events into manageable portions and to picture the positive, when my brain wants to picture the negative.

I notice that I'm more comfortable living in the questions. I'm more and more open to acceptance of reality, trying to just gently hold possibilities. Just … let it be. I cannot always change the outer circumstances, but the choice to serenity is always an internal one.

PRESENCE

Joining Humanity

What joined me more closely to humanity? My own losses, my own failures, my own desolation. While the temptation beckoned to me to flee the death of loved ones that came so close upon each other, somehow I knew that I needed to stay with that brokenness, not run from it or cover it over. Loss can close as well as open the heart.

I began to look in the eyes of strangers and see that same need to cry, the same need to feel comfort. I sat in rooms with other suffering human beings and began to lose that childish need to be somebody deserving of special treatment, immune to the slings and arrows that others suffer. I saw that hurt was universal and that we were all connected, not so much by ease and pleasure in this life but the very situations that made us bleed inside. That and only that connected me to reality and the healing began and continues until today.

It was like seeing the sun rise with a new pair of eyes. I became aware of what the word compassion truly meant: to suffer with, to be willing to shoulder some of another's pain. Not to take over or supply answers, but to truly feel another's pain in the innermost chambers of the heart.

It's not that pleasure can't join us to others, it does. But the level of connection goes deep with the recognition of and empathy with pain.

Ram Doss said, "We are all just walking each other home."

Roger Housden said it this way, "We are all on our way to the exit door."

What a comfort to know we are not alone. We will never be all alone.

Explanations

I wonder if other people at one time or another wonder how the next transition, the passing of our life, will be. Will we retain our personality, will we be cast into another role more exotic or pass into poverty? And the big question – will I meet loved ones again on the other side.

That question opens up a cauldron of queries: Will the pre-deceased recognize me? Will my ex-spouse know who I am and if so, will he/she still be at odds with me about certain things?

And then comes the question of explanations. Will I have to explain my actions while on earth to these people? Wow, that's a big one.

I don't know one completely, perfectly honest person alive. Nor can all of us explain our actions at all times. I do know this: that the more explanations I offer, the more power I give away. For instance, "I can't come to the event because … then comes two or three reasons. I've found that the sentence should end at, "I can't come to the event." Period. Maybe a "Sorry" before or after the decline.

Most of us probably have one friend or more who when meeting starts a barrage of questions to be answered before "Hello" has totally passed their lips. I almost freeze inside when confronted by one acquaintance. I'm instantly transformed to the witness stand at the sight of her. She aims her mouth at me and in rapid fire wants details of my trip, where I ate, where I stayed and what it was like. I can't describe the place I stayed, remember where I ate, nor the particular dish I had.

I'm learning to answer an invasive question by returning that question. "Who are you going to be with for Thanksgiving?" will be answered with, "And who will you be seeing for Thanksgiving?"

Another way to handle excessive questions is to gaze tranquilly at the questioner with a gentle smile and say nothing. I will then be considered senile and hard of hearing. The lapse of time will take care of any repeat questions.

Two Versions

There is a me who is kind, truthful, forgiving and wise. Then there is the me that is sometimes judgmental and selfish. I live with both of them.

I love a comment of Garrison Keillor. He says, "I believe in looking reality straight in the eye and denying it." That's me to a tee sometimes.

A Native American story tells about a grandfather talking to his grandson. He says that there is a battle going on between two wolves inside of all of us. One is full of anger, envy, greed and resentment. The other kindness, empathy, truth and love. "Which one wins?" asks the grandson. The grandfather replies, "The one you feed."

As a young mother with too much on her plate, many times I felt overwhelmed. I didn't want to be either wolf. Mostly, I just wanted to be alone, for a day, maybe just an hour, ten minutes to breathe, collect myself, sort things out.

My greatest pleasure and pastime growing up was day dreaming, writing stories, inventing scenarios for plays. It can be looked at as fortunate or unfortunate but my brother and I mainly raised ourselves. I had the usual dancing classes and piano lessons, but we had long hours of play with neighborhood friends. We rode bikes, built forts, had clubs, made up things to do outside the house. It was good; it was healthy.

Along came grown up time, maturity. With that came the intrusion of life and its vicissitudes. With that came the wolf of discontent. Fortunately, I don't remember this wolf being a hefty one, it had a small stature. Still, it existed. It intruded upon my past dreamy self. Because feelings were not honored in those days, I just stuffed them down inside. The dark wolf was fed from unspoken left-overs.

Still, I sought the good wolf because I liked the way I felt with that energy. I still do. I like the warmth I receive from this wolf, these positive expressions. I like giving smiles from a genuine source inside, whether it be friend or stranger. Just lifting the corners of my mouth at another and receiving a copy of the same, makes life that much easier for both of us.

I'm feeding the good wolf as many meals a day as he can absorb!

Fish

Think of a fish swimming in a glass bowl and then think of a fish swimming in a lake.

The fish in the bowl is safe. It's not subject to being deceived and yanked out of existence. Whereas the fish swimming in a lake is vulnerable to every one of nature's and man's actions. It can be rushed along its path by a storm and it is always open to mankind's fishing pole.

But for the fish in the lake it's probably a "Wow, look at that" or "Whoopee, another rapids" kind of existence. Whereas the fish in the bowl makes the same circle over and over. It can see out on the same view and is protected from the unexpected.

Relating this to people, it might be tempting to stay in one place where we are comfortable, where we've built our nest. And it's tempting to limit contact with others who might disturb this illusion of safety.

I found that limiting possibilities in this way while offering some protection also limits the capacity to feel joy. By closing the door on possible hurt, I also close the door on experiencing delight.

This awareness only becames possible with some kind of shock where I have to open the door. In order to put a new idea inside, an old one has to go. And for me, at least, this process unfolds usually with some kind of event that shakes the old foundation. Some piece of the egoist personality has to crack. It's usually a revelation of a part of us that becomes exposed and we are forced to face our shadow self, something everyone has, and few want to explore.

It's a blessing and relief, this exposure. No more can be expected of us than we are capable of providing. Guilt, manmade emotion, can be thrown out the window. Maybe it's aging, but I am no longer willing to dance to the tune of who another thinks I should be. My goal is to remain loving and caring and to pass kindnesses on, pay it forward, as they say.

Skating on Ice

Watching professional ice skaters is one of my favorite things to do. It's just lovely to see. I can remember taking ice skating lessons with my two daughters. I could be having a day of harassment out in the world, but on the ice with the music flowing, I felt free and light as a feather. I loved watching my girls feel the same thing, once we all found our balance.

One coach's advice just before his student preformed in a competition was this:

1.) Turn off the mind. Let go of all thoughts.

2.) Be in the moment.

3.) Just let the body to respond to the music.

(And oh, yes, stay upright!)

Ice skating lessons with my daughters was joy. Their movements and my movements on ice surprised me with the grace that the body is capable of, rounding a corner, skate over skate, and the smooth reversal to skate backwards.

It was almost a spiritual experience in those busy days of raising a family. It was definitely a happy experience of being in the now with my girls.

Being Here, Now

A man takes his grown son and that son's family on a cruise to Hawaii. Everyone is excited. Much thought has gone into the planning. Now they are on the ship where the entertainment is extraordinary and ongoing, even through the night. Excitement abounds with the children and their grandfather.

The man sees that his two grandchildren are into exploration of the entire ship, entering into the games and enjoying sodas and all the food which seems to have been created just for them. Their enthusiasm is unlimited.

Whenever he sees his grown son, however, the son usually has his iPhone out, texting.

The days go by, and the iPhone consumes most of the son's attention. He's not into playing games with his children, or into enjoying the different restaurants aboard ship. The night stage shows, the art shows, even the adult gambling casinos hold no particular interest.

This man knows his son has never been on a cruise before, so it's not boredom he is engaged in. He doesn't have the money to be taking this trip, he doesn't have extra money for things of this sort for his children. This grandfather is also saving money for these children's college.

This lack of attention begins to annoy the grandfather and he mentions that he wishes his son would put away his phone. But nothing changes. The behavior continues unabated.

Visions of throwing the phone overboard haunt the grandfather.

Finally, after the third day on the ocean, the man has had it. "Son, You are wasting what is most likely a trip of your life time with your children. Now, I want you to put that phone away for the duration of this trip. I want you to *be here, now*…for there won't be another *here, now*. Happy to say, the son honored the request.

Worthy or Not Worthy

James Finley says, "Love is not determined on the worthiness of the receiver. It is determined by the giver."

And I think, who is worthy of love? Are any of us worthy of that gift, or is it just that – a gift.

I believe that was the point of the message, that most of us do not recognize that we are already deeply loved and forgiven by God and there is nothing we can do to earn it – no studying of books, no actions of valor. To one and all it is a given. I liken it to a question: If someone hands you a fifty dollar bill, what do you have to do to receive it? The answer is just reach out and take it. That seems too easy, doesn't it?

I wonder why most of us spend a lifetime trying to love ourselves as openly as God loves us. The major lesson Jesus asks us to absorb is "Love your neighbor as yourself." For some of us we'd have to honestly and with humor add, "Poor neighbor" for we inevitably dislike ourselves, which is so contrary to God's wish. It's easy to be the biggest critic of ourselves. So many times I catch myself with a critical thought about something I "should have done" or something I "could have done." Sometimes it seems we fight to hang onto our poor opinion of ourselves.

Once when I said something about deeply wishing I had done something different, a wonderful friend, Dee, said, "You would have if you could have. But you couldn't, so you didn't." Or another version,

"You would if you could, but you can't, so you don't." The behavior of our youth seldom lives up to the values that emerge as we grow up and mature. Beating up on ourselves helps no one, least of all ourselves.

Richard Rohr says, "We do not think ourselves into a new way of living. We love ourselves into a new way of thinking."

I believe what gets us into trouble is an illusion. The illusion that all our efforts should be 100 percent and that such is doable and possible. I remember the giant relief when I realized that the expectation of perfection could destroy whatever joy could be wrung from life. Whew…that in itself was a gift.

More and more I realize that the ropes with which I bind myself are just that – self-inflicted restraints. I think dealing directly with grief freed me immensely from the illusions of perfection and allowed me to treat myself gently, talk to myself with the compassion I'd offer a good friend. I am the one and only person who will never leave me. I decided I'd become my own best friend. And I like that.

Presence

He has such presence we say, meaning the person we're describing has a certain calmness in his bearing. The state of being totally present is not that common, nor can it be faked. It is being in this very moment, right here, right now.

The mind is never without a thought. Few, and this includes me, spend time in touch with the here and now because it feels like nothing – no thing. There is no competition, no results, no product to display.

You know the saying, "I wish you peace of mind?" Richard Rohr says that this is precisely where peace does *not* reside, in the mind. I think this is because the mind replays the stings of the past. And when it is not occupied there, it casts its pall upon a mostly fearful future: "I am approaching bankruptcy, feel a cold coming on, have lost my friends, and find I have shortness of breath" the mind can tell us, and this when we wake up in the morning before even one foot is on the floor!

My awareness of my own preoccupation with the past or future came to me through some tough times. When I lost two of my children everything was stripped down to nothing, my world was shaken to the core. Going through the grief process I found that the only place I felt a measure of ease was by staying right in the now, minute by minute.

To stay in the present I have to be detached from my mind patterns, addiction to my thoughts, which we all have. This detachment can happen when we are confronted with the death of loved ones, or conversely, when we fall in love. Remember the delightful state of being in love? In that state we lose the need to control things and people. We ease into freedom, lightness, kindness, and the feeling of joy. Life is here. Life is now. And we are fully awake, fully present.

I've developed a practice which allows me peace. Every morning for 20 minutes I close my eyes, pay attention to my breath, and just let myself "be." The mind is never without a thought, so when a thought appears, mentally I've been taught to send it down the river. I don't fight my thoughts, nor judge them. I simply say, "That thought is another leaf," and down the slow, smooth current of the river it goes. This practice, which I fail to practice adequately, was taught to me by Father Richard Rohr and Father Keating. It is simple, direct and when I attempt this it helps me focus on "the now."

And before I practice this emptying of my mind, I ask for direction. My dependence upon my God is unfolding the most amazing, beautiful, safe countryside inside of my being. Here in this state I am Present.

Sharing

There's an ad on television showing two friends hugging without touching, a hair dresser styling someone's hair with the brush four inches from the hair, a woman going through the motions of pushing her daughter on a swing, and a man brushing a dog without touching. It's an ad for avoidance of germs in the flu season.

I laugh at these scenes because it looks so odd but it also appears sad.

Sad because of all the things that keep me going from day to day it's connection, touch, and communication.

I can't imagine greeting a good friend whom I haven't seen in a while with my body a foot away. I want to feel that hug, squeeze that friend with joy. Human touch is one of the things that gives me the assurance needed for facing the day. It's the assurance I do exist and makes possible my contribution to the lives of others.

Touch is healing. The hand was designed not only in order to function daily, but also to convey feelings of warmth and love. And it does just that. Who hasn't had a headache massaged away by a gentle touch? The best of all touch which reaches deep inside is a good laugh. It massages and opens up the whole body, freeing it from tension.

It's hard to imagine being a lone lighthouse keeper. It must take a certain strength, a need for solitude that many do not possess. For that line of work it must take tremendous courage. My need for connection is too strong for me to imagine being in this situation.

And I welcome this need.

Now, Now is the Time...

Fully mature now I'm thinking "yes!" to the idea from Louis Kronenberger when he says, "In our elder years is an excellent time for outrage. My goal is to say or do at least one outrageous thing every week." I love that idea, as long as it's not illegal and brings no harm to anyone.

It's stepping forward. I admit I've always loved a certain amount of irreverence, (letting go of "play pretend") which I translate as being honest, being real.

"Now is time to be dangerous – means dangerously fun-loving, dangerously honest, dangerously involved and dangerously alive" so says Joan Chittister in her book, *The Gift of Years.*

I think it's time to give the inner child full rein, let her whoop and holler, skip and play. If not now, when? From observation I believe some people have been insulted out of their childhood.

I have always startled people with my candor, more and more as the years go by. To say it like it really is proves to be a very soul satisfying act of courage after a youth spent trying to fit everyone's expectations into my own equally valid self. Acutely aware from childhood of other's moods I did not identify feelings in myself until much later in life.

To the question asked to me by a wise and popular writer/speaker/spiritual guide, John Bradshaw, "What do you want,

Tricia?" I had no answer, not the slightest idea. I could tell you what others wanted, but not what I wanted.

Joan Chittister says, "Most of all tomorrow is for living, not for simply ambling around through life waiting to die. A blessing of these years is to give another whole meaning to what it is to be alive, to be ourselves, to be full of life. Our own life."

Expect It, Receive It

What you expect, generally you receive. It's not specifics we are talking about with these four words. It's a practiced attitude of expectation. Whether we are aware of it or not, we have expectations every time we make a decision, do a job, meet a friend for lunch. Why not have positive thoughts rather than negative? I believe that through the years our attitudes become etched upon our bodies and our faces. I also believe that as individual souls there is an invisible but potent aura we surround ourselves in, either "I'm open" or "I'm closed."

Thus, we draw in what we expect.

There is also a truism in the saying, "Expectations are resentments in waiting."

That has validity also. But all depends upon what those expectations are. Trying to practice what some call a Zen mode, I try to shift into neutral when I think about a coming event or possibility. This is not always possible, but at least I'm aware of this choice.

Many times people find me and present a crisis-drama for me to hopefully solve. My response can be to get involved with the dilemma, or I can choose to be responsive but excuse myself from acting the judge on what they should do.

I grew up being the rock in the family, the stable one, the "good one." And there was usually the expectation that I have answers. I tried my best to do just that, always having a suggestion. But as I discovered later on, if these helpful ideas boomeranged, if they were not successful, there was unspoken blame placed upon my suggestion. Their problem was still the same. Seeing life in metaphors, I soon saw that there are certain people who look for open folks and plug into them. Like a giant vacuum, they suck strength from you and usually come back for more.

So, now I am better at putting up reasonable boundaries. It's quite okay to protect myself.

I am projecting, hopefully, the expectation that I am open as always but open to healthy encounters. And I've noticed that is what I am receiving more and more.

Balance

I love remembering the times I spent in the Texas hill country, by the waters of the Guadalupe River. This is where I learned to swim, canoe, ride a horse and bond with fellow campers. This is where I made lasting friendships. Printed indelibly in my mind is the comfort of the slow, gentle and buoyant current of the river. In adult life I continue to visit this soothing scene whenever I can.

I returned to this scene after the death of my son. I lay on a float in the river and let its tender current wash away my tears and begin the healing of my aching heart. On another trip I sat by the river and watched autumn leaves float along. Noticing one yellow leaf in particular, I saw that it continued its journey without interruption because it was floating in the middle of the river. Other brilliant leaves got caught along the way because they were too close to the river banks. They got trapped in the sticks and debris or captured in the huge toes of the large sycamore trees that banked the river.

Nature's lesson: Be neither too rigid nor too loose in life. Try to see both sides of things. And above all, strive for balance.

Easy to say. Hard to do. I was brought up in an era when things were black or white, right or wrong, good or bad. No in between. My father, a successful business man, thought this way, as did almost everyone. I accepted this as the norm while even as a young adult I wondered about the results of being either for or against, the cause of so much strife and warring, misunderstandings and division among people. At that time I was afraid to voice questions. Why wasn't compromise possible where there was a little right here, and also a little right there?

These days I'm looking to include instead of exclude. I just feel better that way.

Train to Tomorrow

I'm sitting here with images and pictures running through my mind, chores to be done, connections to be made, and all I think of is that I need to write ...something...anything. I just need to write, an urgent inner force. Why? Because writing is like taking my brain and running it through a soap and water cycle – a cleansing of the dust and motes that cloud my view.

This morning I'm thinking about trains. Not real trains but vehicles bearing us into either the past or the future. Emotions, old and used, battered and bruised flood my being some days. When I get on the train to yesterday *shoulds and oughts* come out of the blue to attack me. The parental tapes embedded deep in my head float around with a shaking finger of blame. These are not something a mean parent has intended, but I believe that most children continue to see their parents at their most inexperienced, impatient self. It's easier for human nature to embellish the negative.

Getting on the train to tomorrow presents its own set of problems. Again the precious moments of right now fade into a black and white print in my mind, the cargo being one of dread, instead of hope. Planning the ultimate ending of anything is a losing game. It precludes God's plan. And trying to force conclusions throws me into states of uncertainty and resentment.

I'm most content when I become aware of this habit enough to change my thoughts back to right now. With each passing year I find I am able to fully accept the gift of love without trying to change it, figure it out, without trying to force it somewhere it can't go. An honest relaxation into the now presents true freedom – to be and let others be.

Comfort Zones

I am most comfortable in loafers or tennis shoes, carrying books in my arms, walking on a school campus. The comfort has nothing to do with age. It has to do with the excitement of learning. The sole requirement for this comfort is interest.

There is a particular smell to academic halls. The welcome scent of pencil shavings, chalk, and notebooks. The worn steps to the next floor are well traveled, here and there a pen dropped, an empty gum wrapper, the abandoned bookmark. There is always a hint of movement, a path going somewhere.

Learning is akin to being in front of many doors in a hall. All the doors lead to the adventure of learning and the very "not knowing" is the challenge which fuels the experience.

A comfort vision I never tire of is watching the snow fall. Like people, each snowfall is different from the previous one. Some snow issues from the sky in a heavy torrent, wind blowing the snow in a horizontal line; some snow falls gently from the sky, each flake a tiny star; other snowfalls swirl silently on their way to the ground, lazy on their journey. There is something in falling snow that is so gentle, cleansing, and pure. Snow covers the scars of the streets and drapes the evergreen trees in patterns of lace. A veil of peaceful silence prevails as the snow covers a city.

Mountains offer me comfort, solidarity and a feeling of permanency. The mountains were there yesterday, they are here today, and they will be there tomorrow. Towering sights that raise themselves up to touch the sky. These vistas of clarity offer me perspective on my life, problems take on their proper shape. To look as far as the eye can see and observe the distant mountains rests my eyes and mind. Looking from Denver over the entire Front Range I see Long's Peak near Estes Park, appearing stately, jutting up in splendid isolation; Mt. Evans, arms spread wide to embrace the city of Denver; and Pikes Peak looming massive, giant, impressive, presiding over Colorado Springs.

When my children were young, comfort was found being together at our lake house, and a profound sense of comfort in their teen age years when everyone was safely tucked into their beds.

I felt a high level of comfort just being with my children, and later on my grandchildren. I love their openness, their candor and innocence, for children are precious in their insights, often full of wisdom. Honesty is the key to open their doors. Children see much of what is not spoken. And their imagination has no limit.

To be in the sky is comfort to me. The thrill of take-off in an airplane never loses its excitement. There is a moment, a pause, and then all levers are pushed to full throttle, and the plane gathers momentum. Straining mightily, the huge iron bird ends the suspense and lifts effortlessly into the sky. It is like life. Courage, a questing spirit, and trust are the necessary ingredients for full flight. I have taken flying lessons in a small Cessna. And the thrill of the takeoff is always the same. I am a participant in the miracle of flight – the miracle birds experience every day.

I can take flight from the static, and from harsh reality in other ways. Music is another kind of flight for me, it releases the energy of joy, of sadness, of pain and of exhilaration. I dance in my being to the swell of instruments. Music permits the soul to soar.

When I need a quiet heart and mind, being in nature or sitting quietly in a church brings peace. It isn't the message on Sundays, it's more the safety and calm. The presence of my God is felt strongly and that is all I need.

One of the most pleasant zones of comfort for me is wandering in the fields of language and words, playing endlessly with meanings, changing the flow of words, listening for the melody. Moving symbols around in different configurations, inserting metaphors, opening up dead-end ideas – giving thoughts their freedom, giving them a "voice" is pleasure beyond measure. Words have power. They can hurt and sting, but they can also affirm and lift our thoughts. Writing can be the gift we leave for others, the priceless legacy of our uniqueness. It is like leaving our individual thumbprint for the next generation. It is a map of our path through life.

The ultimate in writing comes when we share this with others. When some anonymous person reads our words and feels a kinship with us, feels the desire to talk to the author, certain that at a deep level there will be connection and understanding. The joy of finding that person who is lifted, who feels understood themselves, is worth the risk of putting our thoughts and emotions on paper.

A last important area of comfort for me is sharing with others. Sharing not only pain, but joy and a measure of accomplishment in living with the questions of life. People are more alike than different. There are only so many patterns of emotions and experience. Hearing a like emotion expressed relieves the pain of isolation.

A comfort lies in cutting a piece of my life material to exchange with you. In that trade, we can weave ourselves a beautiful garment from many other human beings and their experiences. We can leave others with a piece of our life experience. In sharing ourselves, we extend and stretch our comfort zones, we create a chain of life with others.

CONNECTIONS

Attachment

"We get angry when we become attached to our thoughts that appear before investigation. We absolutely believe this thought of ours." I wrote this sentence down, its source being Richard Rohr. The wisdom remains potent to me. At times we all become addicted to our thoughts and without checking it out sometimes we are led down a path of untruth.

Say that I'm sad because I'm attached to the thought that you don't care for me. I depend upon clues and unspoken gestures instead of asking for information from you. And when the information is not forthcoming, I am hurt.

Why is it that a simple question for clarification can be so hard to pose? It's hard because I am afraid to ask for what I need. I learned early on that instead of being direct it was less risky to guess, wonder, and hope, and not cause any waves.

It was easier to expect that people could read my mind. Surely if they knew me and loved me, they would naturally understand me. Surprise – they do not. Like a beam that guides an airplane to an airport in a storm, I assumed that a sense of connection would assure understanding. In a small plane at times, one has to pick up the microphone and ask for information and direction. We wouldn't hesitate to do this while flying an airplane, but it doesn't occur to most of us to do this in our personal lives.

In a more mature phase of life, I am finding the risk of asking for what I need less threatening. It's more like telling instead of asking, a statement instead of a question. It's simply saying out loud our hopes and needs, "I'd like more information." Also "I'd like a hug right now" is a simple, clear statement that has no double meaning.

Finally I realized that timidity in later life doesn't make sense. There isn't time to sit and wonder and hope that I will be understood. Nor is there time to waste in waiting to be acknowledged. My patience for being invisible, for suffering in silence is mostly gone by now. I don't tolerate guessing games today. If my request is not possible, I need to know. Simple process but difficult, especially with close loved ones. Years of growing up guessing carves a path in behavior that is hard to change later. The needle on the record keeps falling into the deepest groove.

Awareness followed by action carves a new, healthier groove in relationships.

Our Past

I don't know who said this or where I read it but the idea stuck firmly in my mind: "We are prepared by our past, not destroyed by our past. Don't base your future on your past."

Some lucky people may dispute that because they had one of those "perfect families" growing up. But I believe the majority of people grew up with families having human flaws of one kind or another. Actually, the ones who insist their past was one of perfection might, just might, have a mindset of what is called denial. The deliberate ignorance of reality cripples in the long run. I've lived in the denial house and I've lived in the reality house and at some really tough times I thought denial was indeed the better way to go. But of course I woke up, I grew up.

We are the authors of our lives, no one else. It's easy to place the blame on others for the way life has turned out. But maturity, if reached, points out the fallacy of placing blame on others. There was always a choice. Some of us just make errors in judgment which compounded, result in a path we blame God or our parents for. Most of us have done that.

A better word for this healthy need for reality in the second half of life might be detachment. This lesson is finally surfacing for me. I simply can no longer have a finger in every pie. The need to fix, to change, to control and improve things for others simply fades away with the heavy footprint of truth. With relief I find I don't need to know certain things in family member's lives. I've come to recognize the stain of victimhood that some put themselves into, situations that I cannot change for them.

My only regret is that I did not discover earlier the gem that was hidden in what appears to be failure. And again that which is hidden in the tragedy of loss, the gem I dug for, and that proved to be a life saver. When I asked my creator for guidance and help, the lessons and their gifts appeared because I was accountable, open and ready. At the bottom of my own resources I was finally good soil for the help from on high that has always been available.

Who Are You?

We are so accustomed to disguise ourselves to others, that in the end, we become disguised to ourselves.

Francois de La Rochefoucauld

In a song of old, *Smile*, Tony Bennet advises us to

Smile though your heart is aching;
Smile even though it's breaking.
When there are clouds in the sky,
You'll get by, if you just smile.

I don't know about you, but I definitely grew up smiling, no matter how much I hurt inside. We did not expose our sad side, and finally we did not even recognize what our feelings were. In my family there was the promise of reward for my smiles. There was a taint of shame around feelings. We were taught that what we concretely saw in the world was all there was. Even that thought today brings with it a mental picture to me of dry, arid, blank space.

I remember one evening event in my childhood – me as a little girl – padding downstairs to my parents, who were entertaining, to announce, "I'm scared." The immediate response of my mother was, "No, you're not. Now go on back up to bed, honey." I climbed back up the stairs thinking, "I could have sworn I was scared."

I've been searching all my life for essence. The person beneath the clothes. The spirit of a person. The spirit of myself. The more I search, the more I turn loose of preconceived ideas, the more my own individual spirit emerges. I'm learning who lives under this skin.

And I like her. I like her spirit, I like her courage and I like her continuing interest in the world about her. This person finally is real. She can act from that base.

I wonder why it takes living most of one's life to recognize depth of being and that everything doesn't all depend upon me, that the world revolves around each and every one of us, that our problems are mostly the same. It's how we react to those problems that counts.

I believe we all have a set base line to which we return. We may have ups and downs, but most of us return to our base. I'm fortunate to have a base which is mostly positive. I'm not sure everyone wants to bounce back. Many become comfortable with lower expectations upon the self.

Give me hope! Give me promise! Give me reality!

Connection

For me the secret to life can be summed up in one word: connection. For me, staying alone with my fickle mind is not a good idea. The need to discover who one is depends upon honest feedback from another person or persons.

Teachers have said, "We are so much more than we believe we are." Most of us live life unconscious. The information in books only touches the surface. The deeper consciousness is connected to our spirit, this spreads into nature itself. Animals, birds, trees have consciousness – existing on a different level.

We are so much more than our little circumstances. They do not define us. When I let go of the small self and its surface concerns, I fall into my real life. When I connect with the feeling of oneness with all, when I connect with the wider circle of life, it resides not in my brain but in my soul.

I watch to my surprise the grandness of life turning into wonder and awe at its pure beauty. For me it's about connection. That pristine, clear lifting of the soul - that moment in time - doesn't last, but once experienced, the memory sticks.

I can sit by myself and grieve the petty annoyances, tell myself that things will never get better, but I've learned by this time of life that if I stay in my mind by myself it is a dangerous place to be, an unproductive place to be. The mind's captain is ego and ego has a destructive pull into the negative. The feeling of being special, different and unique will lead us straight into expectation, disappointment and resentment, or so I've found.

I welcome the unknowable these days. I trust in the power of the unseen. Without the willingness to be at ease with the questions, my connection to life is diminished.

Listening/Hearing

The difference between listening and hearing is huge. As a child, before having the experience of the zoo, I remember being told how big a lion could be. But I could not hear in 3-D.

Being born in the desert and loving the desert all my life, I internally identified with the expansive beauty of the Grand Canyon. Then I saw it in person. I drew in my breath. It was like a prayer, the huge physical expression of God's infinite love which spoke to me through the sun and the wind.

In midlife our family joined a new church. I listened to the minister's words as I usually listened to a sermon: attentive but not riveted. However, I had a crisis going on inside of myself at that time. This crisis was met with a complete shake-up of my old ideas. It was a total realignment within me.

As I opened myself in the new church, I heard our minister's beautiful sermons with new ears. I not only listened, I heard in 3-D. I understood his message. I "got it."

I was told Bible stories as a child in Sunday School and later taught for four years those same Sunday School stories to other little children. But it wasn't until midlife that those stories made any sense. As a child I had no personal experience with which to incorporate the tales. But being in crisis, my mind opened. For the farmer who is planting, some of the seeds that fall on rocks do not bloom, but from

71

the seeds that fall on fertile soil much is harvested. Now I heard – if I am walking around bitter and discontent, no positive things can come from that soil. But if I have filled my life with love, every day gratitude for blessings bestowed, then much shall be gathered.

The tight bud of listening usually only opens up to hearing after the heart has been engaged by a shock which brings our assumed game plans to a halt. Something has to shake up the same-as-usual thinking pattern. The shell has to crack for the baby bird to emerge. What seems at first too painful to endure, turns into a blessing if we are open to it.

"S' Wonderful"

"S'wonderful, S'marvolous that you should care for me. S'awful nice, S'paradise, S'what I love to see."

I hummed along as I folded clothes. When I looked up at the image on the TV however, I was shocked. There on the full screen was a beautiful house with flames of fire bursting out of windows and eating up the roof. Meanwhile, the catchy dance tune played on in the background. As the song continued, one saw the flames gradually disappear and the house looked as before. It was an insurance ad.

The initial feeling from this ad was confusion yet somehow familiar.

The evidence on the screen contradicted by the bright and sunny song triggered a great deal of irritation and a real discomfort in me. Nothing was wrong here, the music assured me, while before my eyes a house burned down. How like life. When I was growing up this play-pretend was a staple of the culture. Pretend it's nice, and it is nice.

Time and again I was to be confounded by the grown up's pretension that things were fine when it was obvious, at least to me, that they weren't. This attitude puzzled me as a child. It was like someone handing me a black Marks-A-Lot and telling me, "Now go ahead and color the car red." Grownups are always right, I thought. What they say must be the truth, and so I questioned my own reality time and again.

What a wonderful day when I realized that my observations were right on target more than half the time. I learned to trust myself, my senses and my intuition. I began to interpret life through my own lenses, establishing personal contact with the reality before me. What a relief to recognize the connection of sight, sound, feeling, mind, and body. That it was all of one piece, not separated, not split. The word Holy means whole, of one piece. The price one pays to maintain illusion is one's self.

There is a solid quality to life, a congruence, a genuineness that comes with applying my own truth to my life that comes with seeing beneath what is presented to connect with reality.

Flight

One of Joel Osteen's popular TV Sunday morning talks compared people in our lives to the activity of "flight." Pilots know the words well: there is Lift – Thrust – Weight – and Drag.

I can't remember who said this, but it rang true for me:

"People don't remember what you said. They don't remember what you did. But they do remember how you made them feel."

We all have people in our lives who "lift" us. After we have been with them we feel lifted into joy and well-being. Those people are a treasure to keep. As most of us spend a lot of mental time in judgment of ourselves, comparing our insides with other people's outsides, these people restore our perspective, tear away the illusion that we are somehow lacking the good qualities that others seem to have.

Then there are people who somehow "thrust" us into action. They push us toward a goal, toward the future. These people encourage the best in us to take precedence over past mistakes. They open vast images of a positive future. We all need someone in our lives to whom we can express all our emotions and say our regrets out loud. If these confidences fall upon safe, kind and loving ears, the feelings of relief and forgiveness blend and leave us feeling free somehow. These people radiate healing energy.

There are the inevitable "weights" in life most of us experience where we try again and again to lift these unhappy people into the relief that they neither want nor work for. Sometimes the sense of being responsible for another's happiness is placed upon the shoulders of a loved one. The burden never lets up. It never gets better. The more that is given, the more pressure to give still more. There is never enough. It might be called an addiction in the unhappy one to control, and a compulsion in the other to make the person satisfied, a useless and life draining experience for both.

The same negativity exists in people that "drag" us down. They want to lean upon us, giving us their seemingly unsolvable situations over which they cannot cope. Their expectations create a devastating inner drag upon us.

The good news is that God made us to create wholeness for ourselves in healthy ways. We need to step up and set boundaries. Difficult to do but we need to say, "If you want to stay in the pits, okay, but don't expect me to join you." We need to turn a deaf ear upon the finger of blame and guilt some people will automatically place upon us.

It has taken me a very long time, but I've finally got it that I am in control of very little. It is okay to just be who I am and tend to my own business. What a relief. Today, before being involved by necessity in a conflicting situation, mentally I can put on my spiritual armor. I picture pulling on safety leggings and boots, placing God-protected armor over my chest and head into the fray hopefully with calmness. Being a pilot at heart, mentally I can choose to go into full lift, taking off into a tiny measure of serenity. At times I can do this - sometimes yes, sometimes no. But the knowledge is there, when I choose to use it.

Transformation

There is always a next chapter in life. I've noticed that a major happening occurs about every eight to ten years. Some of the junctures are so smooth that it goes almost unnoticed. Not that any stage is seamless, there is always some little tear in the fabric, some shoe string left undone along the way.

It's a wonder, then, that for most humans it takes us by surprise that a change is made necessary, another road is unavoidably taken in our life. Then the inevitable "why" appears on the horizon. "Why did she leave school; why did he marry so early; why did they have to die?" It's a feeling of unfairness, of being left behind, not chosen in the game.

For some of us, life's storms stir up huge waves. Some totally unpredictable, unruly, destructive event causes the loss of life of a loved one. They leave us abruptly, way too soon. And we bow down in the hurricane wind wondering if we will ever be the same.

There is an undercurrent of strength and indomitable spirit deep inside of us all. I was surprised at the knowledge that I myself am not in control of much, if anything. But there is a humming force in my spirit that can and will be beside me, guiding me with gentle care and comfort if I but ask, if I but let go.

Through loss and tragedy I sensed a golden vein that could be discovered deep inside the mud that was freed only with the total abdication of my own power. In no other way would I have given up control.

I emerged a new person, with the God given grace that I asked for, and received.

There were gifts inside the raw suffering that would never have come about without the presence of that experience. No longer did the question, "Why me?" appear on my horizon. If there be questions that present themselves, I ask of myself, "What," "Where," and "How." What's the next step in recovery, where shall that take place, and how can I share my experience with others going through similar circumstances. It is in that sharing that hope is released in me and in those souls with whom I share.

And that transformation is the gift of unexpected joy.

Who's Speaking

We've long been told to listen to our inner voice. Well and good for some folks. But here is what a lot of us would hear:

"Dummy! Why, oh why did you do that!"

"I think you made a very big mistake in taking this road."

I believe that most wisdom is indeed born of pain. As long as things are going along well, we are feeling good, looking good, and performing mostly well, why would we change our thoughts, reach for a new understanding of anything?

Richard Rohr says that past the age of 30, one learns very little by success. Failures teach us much more. We can only make corrections when we stumble. The human ego will fool itself into thinking that it can do no wrong as long as nothing stops the progression of our desires and wishes. But let a rip in that illusion-fabric happen and a painful awareness that we are not foolproof at all surfaces.

I've met different inner voices at different stages of my life. The little girl voice had an exquisite perception. But it was drowned out by elders who corrected me according to their own experience. I remember picking up clues about people from body language, although I knew not of such a term or condition. I would sense my mother's disappointment by seeing her shoulders slump or just by looking into her eyes. My dad's humor escaped into the room by the same method

– his eyes. Interestingly enough, I can see a light in the eyes of my baby pictures, the same light that is still there today.

As I have added years to this life of mine, I am better at being aware of the inner dialogue I have with myself. I give myself inner hugs with a gentle voice of support today, as well as an actual pat on the shoulder occasionally. And I reach out for a physical hug from friends more today too. It's a nice way to live.

One/Many, I/We

I grew up being trained in "one" style of thinking: there is one place to live, one way to think, one way to make a living, one person in the world who is the perfect mate.

My country was the one; our President was the one; my school was the one. Whatever family, school, or group I belonged to was – the one – the best.

This style seemed natural, everyone I grew up with circling in the same orbit. We thought nothing else mattered in our little world. Then I went off into the grown up world, traveling to other locations, seeing other sights and exposing myself to the many. The experience notches on my belt increased and exploded with new pictures, new visions and new dreams.

In the years between twenty and thirty five my world amplified with marriage and the birth of four children. This graft of experience punched holes in my world of one.

The more years I lived, the more reality bashed into my little world, tearing the seams of "the one." Suddenly I was thrust into a bigger space, and it seemed like overnight, the stars expanded, the edges of life enlarged, and my little world seem to dilate, puff up and amplify. Slowly, slowly the belief systems I'd held so long began to die, or expand and change.

The ten years between fifty and sixty brought a further ripping of the fabric of my fixed-life when I lost my mother, my husband, my son and daughter to death, in increments of every three years. My life shrunk into a fearful, tight ball of one again. Everything circled around pain.

But I fought back and formed connection with other human beings. Some of them were trapped in the agony of grief themselves. Then, slowly, feeding each other spoonfuls of compassion, love, and patience, I found my peace, my sanity existing within the widened pools of the many.

I exchanged my one: me, myself, and I, with we. We – what a difference this made. No longer trapped in the prison of "one," I found a mirror into which I looked: other eyes, other minds, other pain, and found the pool of "we" widening finally into a river of joy. Laugher intruded with its release of tightness – a breath of fresh air. Humor transformed my body and soul and allowed me to enter into a world of comfort at last. Together we can rise above.

Today my life-line is with people. Not just those who march in step with my old self. I find myself enjoying new steps that wander and falter and change directions. I find myself unable to enjoy the old system of repetition. I delight in confronting the world's pronouncement that how it was done in the past is the only way. I delight in seeking out my transformed image of growth and finding in nature as well as people unused paths to take. I continue wandering in God's bounty of beauty, seeking the new, the unusual, the genuine. Including other people of all persuasions, religions, color and creed into my world has enriched the fabric of my life to such an extent that I awaken each day with a zest for surprise!

Where You Want To Go

Sometimes you want to go
Where everybody knows your name.
You want to go where people are glad you came.
You want to be
Where you can see
Our problems are all the same.
You want to go
Where everybody knows your name.

This signature song announced the beginning of every television episode of "Cheers."

It was a program that comforted me in a harsh time of my life.

For me today there is a place inside that can only be filled by being with other people. It may seem at times that I would be just fine if only other folks would leave me alone. But without feedback from caring others, my own counsel can often mislead me.

During remembered past years the relief of contact with other adults always eased my angst and fatigue. While raising a family, just to have one adult conversation during the day loomed as a rare gift. I remember the fun of short comments made with the grocery store checker. The mailman too was treated to inane conversation.

Growing up myself, when family conflicts arose I escaped to my room with my best friends, books. I also dreamed of a possible career as a nun. However, after my shy school years, I found most pleasure with groups of likeminded women with whom I felt at ease and that song *Sometimes you want to go/Where everybody knows your name/And they're always glad you came* still brings a smile to my lips.

Love Appears

Have you ever met a person for the first time and feel as if you are greeting each other again, that somehow you know this person? Roger Housden in his book, *Ten Poems to Open Your Heart,* says that love invites us to allow the possibility that our lives were never entirely in our hands, if indeed at all. Of all things, love is the greatest mystery. Better, then, not to hold fast to certainties about where it came from or where it might lead. Better to be open to enjoy love one day at a time.

Roger Housden says that in Wislawa Szymborska's poem, *Love at First Sight,* she is reminding us that there is a season and a time for things that cannot be orchestrated. You will know the right moment by the ease with which you fall into this next chapter of your life. It will require no effort, just an assenting to what wants to happen.

Love opens our eyes to the probability that our life is not totally in our control, that life arranges things as in a dance, every movement has its own unique rhythm. There are no coincidences. I believe, as Roger Housden believes, that at times certain orbits cross. That there is nothing to contrive, nothing to try to make happen. We don't have to try to orchestrate love, we don't have to orchestrate life. We don't have to force anything. What a relief if we could always live life this way.

With the realization that I can let go of my little mind's set patterns of the way my life should look offers an immense freedom of spirit. I sit and watch the river, it has its own path across the pebbles and rocks. This doesn't mean that I can just sit and watch life with no effort. It means for me to make the plan that seems best at this time, but not to insist on following that particular path if too many road blocks appear. It's an expansive feeling, the freedom to accept the gift, to believe that things occur in their own time, at the right place in our lives. It's all in the letting go of having to be in charge, to be my own God. I always believed in God, but when I let go of my control, fully trusting in his guidance, it opens wide the doors of possibility and hope. It seems that if one doesn't have a God to trust, then one must be one's own God. I needn't even whisper what a disaster that could be for me. And what a responsibility! To be in charge of everything and everybody.

As long as my choices do not impinge upon another's life I am free to embrace the belief that there are movements in life over which I have no control. All I have to do is let it be.

The Third Way

Most of us have heard the old saying that we human beings meet life's troubles by either "fight or flight." We charge ahead or we run away. I believe there is a third way: Wait. It means to take no action. It means to resist reactions of any kind.

It's a normal propensity to charge into situations to try and right them. Like a mobile – when one of the hanging pieces gets askew, the whole mobile gets off kilter. Relationships, especially those in the family, can become difficult. Misunderstandings abound. The immediate response is to challenge the other person or to turn around and leave the scene. At times both of these are an obvious choice but sometimes postponing the reaction is the wisest thing to do.

Of all the challenges in life, not knowing and waiting remains the biggest stumbling blocks to peace of mind. I need to know. I want to know, right now, how things are going to turn out. My not so trustworthy mind tells me all kinds of screw-ups that could occur. It seldom whispers good things to come. This mind pretends to be my friend but I'm aware of its sneaky, negative side that masquerades as brilliance.

It's taken me into midlife to recognize the wisdom of waiting. I've been advised to "turn it over to God" for years. First I wondered, how do I do that? Then I voiced my agreement to do just that, still being unsure of exactly what that means. But life and its problems kept arriving with its load of darkness as well as light. My pitcher of tolerance reached its limit. I finally accepted that by myself I simply could not manage everything. The knowledge of my limitations made its impact on, not just the mind, but my deepest self – in the heart, in the guts. I asked God to take my day and my problems and guide me through it. I will do the foot work but I ask for directions from above. Things seem to evolve in a much better way when I release control in that way.

Lo and Behold, it works. It really does.

The Second Half of Life

In his book, *Finding Meaning in the Second Half of Life*, James Hollis, Ph.D. tells us that the question in the first half of life necessarily is, "What does the world ask of me?" The first half of life is driven by the efforts to feed our ego strength, to acquire recognition of one's community, to succeed in a career.

In the second half of life, James Hollis says we're lucky if we inquire, "What does the soul ask of me?"

Hollis tells us while the first half is driven by the fantasy of acquisition, the second half asks the questions, "What does it mean that I am here? And "Who am I apart from my roles, apart from my history?"

I can remember finding those questions arising in my mind. Who am I apart from the image I've spent a life time forming? Am I really the person my family, friends and community think I am? Do I believe that this image I've built is the deepest me I can attain?

I have pictures of me as a teenager growing up in West Texas sitting quietly in our front yard, gazing at the far away mountains of Mexico, deep in thought. In protection from family arguments and angst over my brother's acting out, I retreated into books, dreams and even a desire to join the quiet peace of a nunnery. So even back in early childhood, I knew that security was found on the inside more than outside in the world.

I know that the ego certainly doesn't want to ask deep questions of me.

It abhors change. It was the emergence of frustration, failure, and loss that asked these questions. The need to let go of old ideas, to ask new, deeper questions of myself was the way out of pain for me. To stop identifying with roles and status was crucial to finding a new path to travel now in this second half of life.

All I know to do at this juncture is to welcome the change, explore the change, and try to appreciate even the losses that accompany aging. The teachers come in strange events and surprising people.

Morning Parade

In the park early this morning I stood and watch geese cross the paved path from one side of the park to the other. There were at least a dozen or so on the march. In the silence of early morning all that could be heard was a gentle slap-slap of webbed feet on the pavement – the flat-footed soldiers marching by. There seemed to be a "general" in the lead, just as in flight, they pattern themselves with a leader. The geese seem to instinctively know that they need an "out front" person to follow.

I speculate whimsically how this selection process might takes place. Do they vote?

As I understand their formation in the sky – first a lead bird, then a v-formation, it is a natural pattern of aerodynamics, the wind of each bird's wings providing lift for the ones behind. There is no fight between them to maintain the lofty position of lead. They just fall into line naturally.

I used to go about my day perfunctorily but now I have become an observer. God provides clues of how life works in the ordinary. God wants me to see him in the everyday events and notice the miracles that constantly appear in nature, wants to be with me in the non-dramatic visions of life. In that way I am spoken to in the least likely of persons, in the always available daily presentations.

I pick up another clue this morning from the geese. There is a group of geese surrounding a pool of water in the path, formed from the sprinkler system. "The morning coffee klatch" I say to myself, as I watch them drink and shrug off water, one bird nudging the other. We need community with others. We can choose to go it alone, but things go easier with sharing.

I smile and thank the geese for their morning lesson.

DISCOVER

Do Nothing

Do you remember the saying of long ago, "Do something! Even it's wrong"? I came from a family of achievement. My dad was a charismatic "can do" person who built his own pipeline business extending to Turkey and abroad. He was also an instigator/promoter of the pressure-weld in laying pipeline.

So, that urge to go forward was encouraged in our family. And we were proud of that.

The good thing was that we were encouraged to be creative and think outside the box.

Today everyone knows the wisdom of pausing before taking action. But how many of us presume whatever the problem is that we can fix or refine it? That urging is strong.

If I have a thought for a friend's situation, without pausing, I say it out loud.

I call this impulse-control or lack of control. I watch stunned as many girlfriends plunge into department stores buying everything that lights up their eyes. Perhaps I'd be one of them except for my dislike of shopping in a mall. That beckoning to buy is like a siren that goes off that certain people can hear. Upon entering Neimans with a friend, I watch her eyes glisten. With her expert guidance over-riding my desire to hurry up, I find myself leaving with a purchase of my own. My friend, expert salesperson in her own right, with her enticing smile urges me to buy something. It's a hat. I don't wear hats – but I went home with one.

There are the situations with family members and friends that set up my effort to make things better for them. I find my voice offering suggestions which were not asked for. I've got an answer for the problem which I plunge right ahead and offer, when the best thing I can do at the time is listen. All in all, a lesson to be repeated daily – *do nothing*, with love.

Steadiness

People buying a home have a guiding principle to remember. It is an important factor in real estate – location, location, location.

An important guide for me is balance, balance in all its aspects, whether reacting to good news or to bad news as well as in every corner of my life. Of course, trying to be balanced in every area is an impossible goal. Things happen and I just react.

But like a child's see-saw in the yard, one end is on the ground, the other end is up, very little balance time. Life in our culture seems to have the same problem. The pendulum at times swings wildly. We go from extreme control to no control – from extreme right to extreme left.

With so many people on diets, I look at this concept of balance. The key to successful dieting seems to lie in portion control, more than denying the self. I notice that at times the size of my meal creeps up slowly until I look at my bowl and discover with amazement enough cereal for a football player. Solution: I've kept my baby grandchildren's tiny little bowls, a picture of a playful elephant on the bottom. That vessel I use for my sweet portion of the day. Everything in moderation is an old saw – for me it comes down to the effort for balance.

Connecting facial expressions to balance, my face happens to be too expressive, one of those that reports exactly what I am feeling. I cannot successfully pull a joke or lie. I'm thinking I could attain balance easier by controlling the expressions on my face. I watch with envy those actors whose faces remain cool and collected in the midst of all circumstances.

On the positive side of having an expressive face, friends and loved ones have no doubt about my genuine affection for them. It literally shines out at them.

Regrets

How many thoughts surface at times about what we wish we could have done and should have done? Those guilt-fetes are useless but regardless, at times they haunt us all.

I can know intellectually what a waste of time this negative thought process is, still before I can spot what's happening, there the specter is again. It usually involves some time in my younger years, before I became awake or aware.

Every one of us, of course, can go back and find many dust balls under the furniture to think about. The "if onlys" hang out there. If only I had done this or done that, if only this had not gone the way it did, on and on the refrain goes.

Finally, if I'm fortunate enough to let in other, objective and wiser thoughts it becomes apparent what a waste it is to think I was ever totally in control of the past. The ability to open the door to wiser observations is usually brought about by the shock of finding myself in a dilemma I cannot solve.

The ego that tells me I don't need the observations of others can run me into the ground. I don't have to believe all my thoughts. In fact, I should question many of them.

"Yes, I'll have that second piece of cake" no, no, no…

"I need to talk to that person, straighten out his thinking" wrong, wrong, wrong.

"She ought to know better!" She doesn't. Get over it.

Expanding our consciousness, examining the way we've always done things and thought things seems to be the core of growing up.

To continue the old way of proving myself right, therefore proving someone else wrong is not only unkind, but turns people away. So also is the opposite, the old way of mea culpa – I'm to blame – forever to blame. This refrain can keep us in bondage to self-hatred and the ego's mistaken idea that we carry much more influence than we actually do. A given that I learned from Richard Rohr is that the harshness with which we judge others begins with a harsh judgment of ourselves. Human beings are expert in self-denigration, putting oneself down. If I can't be the best, I'll just be the worst.

Most of my "want-to-do-overs" were not committed by design, by deliberate thought or deed. I can let go of old guilt-patterns and look to today. Am I kind to others today? Can I give a warm smile, a helpful hand today?

I hope so.

Illusion of Possession

How true the joke: "I never saw a U-Haul following a hearse." Possessions end up possessing us.

All of us know that at some level. But a lot of us let that pimple of possession spread into the arena of human relationships. I remember in high school, if my best friend laughed more with some other friend, if she invited her to come over more often than she did me, I felt bereft like I'd lost something or someone, like I was less than.

It happens in families. Mom or Dad show more appreciation or give more intense attention to one child than another. How difficult being mother and father, handling every little event and occasion with an exact behavior, especially when the facts might be that one or more of the children has a serious illness. When the house is on fire who can measure out in exact amounts the energy of love and concern to everyone, when mere survival is paramount.

I don't believe life has ever been tit for tat. Love over here is not taking love from over there. The illusion that there is only so much love to go around disappears hopefully with maturity.

Love is not contained in a measuring cup to be dispensed evenly. My experience is the more people I include in my circle of love, the more love I experience from others. It's a spilling over of acceptance of the imperfection of others. A sigh: They are not perfect either. It's not easy, this trust. It means I'm willing to open up to you, to be vulnerable before you.

To compete and compare presents the ideology of over/against and is counterproductive. It leads to put downs and misunderstandings. It might be more productive and certainly easier to change from either/or to Yes, And, as Richard Rohr so beautifully states in his book by that title. The situation is this, yes, and also it is that. To live this way is relief from the stress of constant measuring and comparing. In everything that comes along, our choices in life have a light side and also a shadow side.

Peace, stay with me.

Word Power

Seldom do we realize the power of words. I picture compassionate words circling the air. There are many hands stretching to grasp those words, like reaching for stars. Then there are angry, bitter words. No hands reach out for them, there is no soft landing for this string of letters. They hang out there, like icicles.

Words can be softened often just by the tone of voice. "Let it go" can be said with a harsh, hurried tone or it can be said softly, in a lower tone. Inflection on which word is important too. The emphasis can be on the *Let* or *go* marking the importance of the directive.

In today's television, talk is mostly a race. Time is money, and the anchors have to get through much more information than ever before. Some weather persons give the impression that they have very restrictive minutes, even down to the seconds. Before I can study the area in which I live, they are off to another part of the country. I'm sorry, could you repeat that please.

As much as words sway, convince, condemn, offer sympathy, or show love, the absence of words can be powerful too. Did you ever notice when silence can feel like punishment?

If it stretches on and on, the discomfort doubles. There is a difference in the silence between two people who are in tune with one another, are relaxed with each other and the silence contained between two people who don't know each other well or don't trust each other.

We know this intuitively. And few there are who are willing to be vulnerable by sharing what is really going on. A senior friend of mine wrote a whole book to communicate to her family who she had grown to be, desiring to convey truths that couldn't be covered in the short visits across the country. As a matter of fact, that friend is me.

To be a wordsmith is fun. It's like the freedom of a child playing with blocks. One is free to play around with words, change, cut and add to one's heart's desire. Letting the mind wander in the field of metaphors is especially interesting. It's like coming upon new flowers in a field, some surprising connection that only you have managed to see. It feels fresh. It is fresh. It opens a connection with others.

I remain ever so thankful for this gift. And yes, I claim it.

The Cracked Pot

Roger Housden's series, "Ten Poems to Change Your Life" reveals to me how important it is to cherish one's life just as it is. Roger Housden translates all his collection of poems with such clarity. He says of one of the poems, "To praise the imperfect, the ordinary, is not something that comes easily to us in the Western world. But in Japan there is an entire worldview that appreciates the value of the imperfect, unfinished, and faulty. In Japan it is the aesthetic that sees beauty in the humble, the irregular."

I was watering my blooming geraniums, when I noticed a crack in the clay pot and I thought about this view. I had other pots of flowers but this one with the crack displayed the most beautiful flowers. I thought about most humans' belief that if things are not perfect they are more or less useless. We strive for perfection only to fall into disappointment, envy of other's fortune, and the resulting resentment when a flaw appears. It seems to be a given, that this heavy desire for perfection will result in negative emotions.

I know it is comparisons that I stumble over, the constant measuring this against that. When I finally quit this useless game, I came to see that all of us have been given a special gift, our life is unrepeatable and valued just the same as others by the God of our understanding.

What a blessing, what a relief to finally understand that in the end all that is asked of us is to give up mimicking, trying to match others in any way and be as authentic a person as we can be.

Requirements

I was taught from childhood that to be a caretaker was the highest goal for a woman. My trainer was my mother. It was a given, this expectation that became more and more apparent, that I would take care of her feelings and her problems. I was her most important confidant, indeed her "life" she told me many times.

Learning how to be super vigilant concerning others, watchful of their moods, and adjusting myself to ease whatever tense situation I found myself in became the norm for me. I continued doing this "radar job" most of my life with no thought of its consequences.

It was not until later in life that I came to see how exhausting and defeating this task was. But even today, I find myself slipping into the old habit of trying to ease situations for others that feel tense. It is as natural as breathing. The catch-22 of this is that I truly *do* care about others in my life. I care tremendously about their well-being and their happiness. I want the best for my loved ones.

The key for me was the discovery of the amount of arrogance that lies hidden in this way of life. It's fairly simple. I am not God. I do not know always what is best for an individual. It's not I who guides this being on their path of life. I don't know what path they are on or how the God of their understanding will lead them down this path. I don't know where they will be led or in what time frame.

Taking the heavy mantel of responsibility off my shoulders releases the energy for truly being there for a person. I am not responsible for the circumstances in which loved ones find themselves. A card bearing this message is fixed on my refrigerator so I am reminded daily:

Do not feel totally, personally, irrevocably responsible for everything.
That's my job.
Love,
God

I was not prepared for the most important part of parenting – letting go, the releasing of our babies to fly out of the nest and forge their own way through life. The urge to protect and promote their good persists well past the stage of life when we should be released from the duty. I wanted to cling, I found the same admonitions and cautions continuing to flow through my veins and out my mouth.

I've developed a mantra for myself when I visit my grown children and their families today. It is simple. I say to myself: "Nothing is required of you at this time."

While I cannot always remember to do this when there, my intent is to present myself with a heart full of love and try to remain quiet.

It Matters

A quote from jazzman, William Hardy: "Life is like a trumpet. If you put nothing in, you get nothing out."

A good friend of mine, Louise, said, "It doesn't matter what you think, it doesn't matter what you feel. It matters what you do." We can spend time lamenting situations, ruminate over a slight, but what matters most is what we do with this, what we do with the day given to us. How we spend our hours each day.

What I fill my brain with matters. I know that every violent movie I've ever watched lingers in my mind long after I've left the theater. And after seeing visions of terrible illnesses, the next morning I'm going to have a broken spleen, be losing my eye sight, left alone and put into a nursing home – all before my foot hits the ground. Likewise, after a romantic movie, my favorite kind, before I open my eyes the next morning there are two or three calendar firemen standing by in my foyer, waiting for me to arise.

In reality, sitting by the slow current of a river, walking in the park stirs a pleasant center in my being. On my walk I observe a young girl skating, rhythmically moving to the music in her ears, a mother pushing her baby. The smile brought to my face radiates down my whole body. I hear the unusual sound of bag pipes and look around to spot a man practicing under the trees near the lake. I love the surprise that people bring into our lives if we are looking.

Living alone if I stay in my own brain too long, without feedback from another person, I need to bring a flashlight and a gun! A pretty picture does not evolve.

What I consciously do about filling my mind – it's my habit to listen to CDs of spiritual guidance in my car as I do daily routines. I also dance to CD peppy music in my kitchen.

P.S. I don't especially like to cook, but I can move my body on the floor really well. It does matter what thoughts I put into this head, what movements I put in my body.

Another Perception

They say it is easy to get stuck in our perception of those closest to us, that it is easy for people to accept only information that confirms the impressions they already have, to discount any new information counter to that.

We can become strangers to those closest to us. Sometimes we don't inquire for any new information, we aren't curious, don't ask questions.

It's like the childhood game of statue. Someone twirls us around and around, then flings us away. We then freeze in the position in which we land.

This is how it feels when our children and others internalize us, form opinions about us which originated most likely at our most uninformed, floundering young years.

They freeze us in that position. They don't let us grow up, they don't see how much life has changed all of us and helped us grow into responsible, loving and giving people in our own right. Their opinion of us has been set in concrete it appears.

That was then; this is now. Opinions formed early in life sometimes last a life time.

It has been found that until someone undertakes doing their own inner investigation and work, the chance of discovering new facets of those we love is less apt to happen.

If we're lucky, consciousness sometimes leaps forward, like waking up from anesthesia. We look back at some of our certitudes with surprise. "Wow," we say, "The truth is just the opposite."

Some say a clear sign of maturity is being able to listen to and find a kernel of truth in what another is saying – to let those thoughts enter our minds with no prior judgment, to sit with and occasionally ponder an opposite opinion.

Growth and change are usually painful. As someone (I wish I knew who) said, "We cling to known hell, rather than fly to unknown heaven" because that involves no risk.

Trying to separate the self from the pain of life is cutting possible joy in half.

As Rainer Maria Rilke says:

> *Let everything happen to you*
> *Beauty and terror*
> *Just keep going*
> *No feeling is final.*

To Fight or Not

The pain is in the attachment. The stronger the attachment, the higher the level of discomfort when it's challenged. It seems the more I fight situations, the more I cling to what the outcome should be, the more uneasy I become. Someone said, "What we resist, persists." So what should I do? I'm learning to spot ego when I'm feeling hurt. It seems that whenever I feel hurt by someone it is more about where the other person is in their own lives than it is about me. When I get upset it is the ego part of me that feels rejected.

My vocabulary has changed through the years. The things I used to think were my assets have turned out to be defects and the things I thought of with some shame, turned out to be my assets. For example, when I was in my 20s I prided myself on having what I called "my father's drive" in life. Stepping out and telling people how to do things. Getting things done. Fighting the good fight, like my executive father. I was in my 40s before I realize that getting things done my way most likely belonged on the minus side of an inventory. Many times it was nothing more than self-will. I've long known the fact that anger takes a tremendous toll on the body. Our hearts and our minds constrict, and we suffer the cost of friendships and love.

The attributes I felt were weakness turned out to be more on the asset side. I have always had a compassionate, intuitive soft side, naturally thinking the best of people. In error, I saw the unwillingness to be harsh as something weak and incompetent.

As life progressed with all its twists and turns, its problems and danger, and its sudden tragedies, a new way of seeing has surfaced. I find myself taking a breath and waiting.

My choices used to be to jump in and stir things or leave. I could fight or not.

Each time I release the passion to persist when there is an obvious reason not to do so, I find the ground that I stand on is solid. The release that comes from this change in attitude is immediate. The idea of non-resistance quiets and restores my mind and body. Wish I could say I do this all the time. I do not. But I seem to be developing a hesitation to plunge in, a reluctance to fight anything or anyone. While I am not by any means a doormat, I can better pick and choose what battles to fight. They are few.

Recipe

I was Publicity Chairman of the PTA at my children's school, and on a day in September I handed out a chicken spaghetti recipe for the students to take home to their mothers for the school spaghetti dinner. I thought this way we'd avoid the comparison of whose mom was a better cook! When each batch was set out I was surprised that there was so much difference, in taste, in texture, in presentation. One had more salt, one not enough sauce, one in a colorful festive bowl, another in a plastic bowl. Yet the recipe handed out was the same for all.

Those were the days when the goal was to fit into the norm. The closer we resembled one another, the better our children obeyed the rules, the happier we were. Moms wore similar styles in their clothes, cut their hair alike; the dads followed the company line in detail. Those who didn't comply were not admired. They were considered odd or troublemakers.

It took many years for me to trust myself. I simply followed "the thing to do." There was a set pattern for everything. We moms passed the piano teacher's name to our neighbor and we sent our children to the same camps as our tight little group of friends. There was nothing wrong with this. This pattern offered security. We were comfortable with knowing what the next step was. And it was a good starting point. But it wasn't enough somehow for me.

It took many years for me to trust myself and to think for myself. That was when I realized the freedom to seek my own originality offered new strengths and the development of my soul. I had always known there was much more to life than the set molds before me. Knowledge of the inner self in those days was not encouraged; in fact it was discouraged, a set back to last a very long time.

Now I see – our Maker gave most of us the same outside appearance with ten fingers and ten toes. But like the spaghetti recipe, we are free to develop the insides – so much salt and pepper, so much sugar, a bit of this and a bit of that until we are truly an original. Some may prefer to skimp on an ingredient, add more of something else, or just not participate in making anything.

So much for the automatic urge to judge, critique, and measure, to compare and compete. That seems to me to be the recipe for unhappiness. We can let go of the driven desire to look better, perform better, be at the top. What a relief. We can now join our fellow man, and collect a wide variety of friendships like a brilliant jeweled bracelet.

LETTING GO

Leaving Home

Most of us interpret the term "leaving home" to mean a departure from the house in which we grew up. All of us, at one time or another, have moved our body into a different environment, a different roof over our heads – an external leaving.

There is another meaning to the term which I call "internal leaving." It can happen under any roof at any time. This was a necessary step for me in order to reach a deeper meaning for existence.

In Richard Rohr's book, *Falling Upward*, he talks about the necessity to let go of ego-building tactics of the first half of life, to turn away from the "win-lose, measure against" ideal. As Rohr indicates, in the first stage of life, decisions mostly depend upon either/or thinking. This is necessary throughout life to plan and manage our days, but it is limiting. Aging necessitates the incorporation of a larger view. This expanded consciousness allows us to "leave home." Although this feels like loss, as Rohr says, "It is often the very birth of the soul." He says we cannot expect the top four inches of our body (our brains) to carry us successfully through midlife without painful repercussions.

James Finley states it another way: "We stop ranking vertically and we start connecting horizontally."

Looking back I can see that I always had an interest in the deeper questions of life and the study of the human psyche. I was drawn further into wisdom teaching by loss. I was in the book store looking for something to read to alleviate the severe pain I was feeling after my husband died. I glanced at the book cart standing in the isle. On top was a book by Richard Rohr, *Job, and the Mystery of Suffering*. That book opened the door to healing for me.

As I had believed, there wasn't some punishment from on high in loss, a blame situation did not exist. How can I turn my losses into something good?

I chose to leave home, the old thinking patterns, and move into an enlarged space. I came to the realization that lost loved ones could be served best by my decision to live life with enthusiasm, joy, and faith as much as I was able.

Age of Answers

It seems like overnight the world went from seeking answers from books and teachers to the age of instant answers just by picking up our iphone and asking our questions to the ever present Siri. You can ask her every kind of question from the sublime to the extremely personal and absurd and voila! She has the answer. She will even mimic human responses like, "Hmmmm, let me think about that."

I, on the other hand, have decided to try and let go of the need for answers. When I can do this it helps immensely with my inner peace. Raising a family of course I was expected to have answers. And I did. This carried over to assisting everybody, about anything.

In middle age, I began a most rewarding occupation, teaching creative writing to adults. I taught memoir for some 14 years and within this frame work my students and I progressed in inner awareness. I opened each class with, "I will be your Co-Pilot, you are the Pilot." My next set of classes centered around Edward R. Murrow's classic radio show of the 50s, *This I Believe.* This fertile field added acres to surprisingly rich spiritual and emotional soil. This was a format in which I could share my own experience which opened the way for others to share theirs comfortably. The class flourished.

With maturity, it became more and more doubtful that having answers was the gift it was purported to be.

I became aware that most of the time with others what was needed was just my presence.

Instead of the need to know, I made a game out of not knowing. No control necessary. What's going to show up today? Deep breath. Just let it be what it wants to be.

Lay Down

The bells of truth ring out in some country western songs. One in particular, *Help Yourself,* sung by Sad Brad Smith has the line, "Wc believe in everything that you can do if you could only lay down your mind."

I'm thinking oh, the things I could do if I could only lay down my mirrors. At this stage in life trying to keep up the appearance of someone younger just occupies too much time. And yes, I recognize the vanity in that. Is it really worth it? No.

Then there is, "Oh, the things I could do if I could only lay down family worries." And if I could only lay down the "I will carry your difficulties for you" sign on my back. Those I barely know sense in me a vulnerability to the suffering of others. They approach and "plug in." Automatically I respond. It takes a while for me to catch on. Then I'm usually pretty involved in the helping game.

Thing is, when does "help" help? I would say rarely, but it depends a lot upon the kind of help. I believe that having answers for everyone while raising a family promotes impulsive answers for everyone thereafter. Becoming more aware now, I practiced before traveling to worrisome destinations. I pack my "box of Ohs." Yes, the collection of "Oh." When I am forced to listen to a litany of woes, my response now is a sympathetic look and one simple "Oh." Game ends. It's like tennis. The opponent sends the ball (problem) over the net.

Naturally the goal in tennis is to return the ball. But with this new awareness, I let the ball (the organ recital of woes) go past me. I stand there with a gentle smile on my face and just let the ball go by. "Oh." The game cannot continue that way. It ends.

And oh, things I could do if I lay down judgments and opinions. Like everyone I have opinions that happen to make perfect sense to me, but I'm aware that it is wise not to try and force my opinions on anyone else. It's like the teaching of creative writing. There are a few rules but the major task is to let go of any rigid ideas or plans and let the juices flow. As the sun goes down it's a pleasant thing to just "lay down my mind."

Letting Go

"Hold on!" "Turn loose!" These pithy reminders are very confusing. When to "hold 'em, when to fold 'em." When to hold on, when to let go presents conflict.

I remember the days of long ago when our family enjoyed water skiing on Lake Travis. We had a little house right on the lake and a blue boat and everyone was learning to water ski. Jeanine learned easily, Carver seemed a pro, Lee an expert. Finally the moment I dreaded came – "Come on, Mom. You can do it too."

Try I did. It was a struggle. I would be gulping deep breaths as I sat in the water, wobbling skis in front of me. Then came the question, "Are you ready?" And a shaky, "Yes..."

The boat would lurch ahead, I would try to lift myself onto the skies and fell backwards every time.

I was also awakening to my own inner strength those days, trying very hard to trust in God, trust in people, trust in myself. Slowly I was finding out that indeed there was a God out there waiting for a simple, "Help." All I had to do was believe, reach out, and let go to this power.

So I decided to try this experiment in learning to water ski. One more time in the water, skies on. Here I am again, trying to water ski which up to now has not worked! I'll try again, one more time.

This time when asked, "Are you ready?" I voiced a "You bet!" to my husband at the wheel of the boat. And then I relaxed, I quit fighting to get up. I simply sat back and let the boat's power bring me out of the water on my skis!

Trusting the power, I let it lift me. What a glorious feeling to be zipping along the water not self-powered, but energy-not-my-own-powered, a higher power.

The Right Opinions aka The Right Ideas

One has not given up all things for God if that person is still holding onto the purse of their own opinions.

St. Francis

Richard Rohr reiterates this idea often. He says, "Our most dangerous riches are not so much material possessions as our attachments to ourselves and our own ideas."

It's strange this brain. It seems to have compartments and nooks and crannies where I store and lock opinions. The mind has many filters, all slanted towards a forgiving mirror of myself. These filters are necessary in young adulthood to assist me in my journeys. But they can trip me up in adulthood.

For me, around middle age, the filters became less rigid. I filter out fewer ideas of others that are different from my own. I let other thoughts come in. Maybe the filters themselves are just plain tired. I know I am. I'm tired of the games people play, myself included, to protect rigid views. I've learned to admit new information even though it might not fit the old pattern, what I once thought was totally right. My early training was to not make waves, to just agree rather than insist upon my own view. Today I'm freer to acknowledge my own views, not insist others follow suit but just hear where I am. To a large extent I have let go of the "disease of please."

It's fun to observe how occasionally grown up and accepting I can be, with little desire to change others. I'm more open to other ideas, at least to listen to them. Frequently now I find reality in another set of opinions and thoughts as well as my own.

I feel I can learn from all opinions, if only that it's not beneficial to me, at this time. It's a comfortable, pleasant way to live.

The Power of "I Don't Know"

Raising a family brought lots of joy along with the necessity to step up and know things, daily answer questions and give directions. Innocence blue eyes searching my own, full of the surety that mother knows. Most mothers do know what safe direction to take at an early stage of their children's lives. So it's easy to continue to believe it is within our power to know what is best. Trouble arises when we continue to do this *knowing* for our children long past when it's needed or wanted. I did that I'm sure. Most mothers do.

I contributed my ideas to friends too, to fellow workers and anybody who presented a problem. All of this has best intentions at its base, we care, we truly do want to help.

I came to be aware of this pattern of expecting myself to have answers when my youngest child became ill. I thoroughly investigated the facts of her illness as far as it was known and had consultation after consultation with the medical community at large and specialists in the field. I prayed nonstop for a solution. But there was only temporary help. And after years it became obvious that I simply did not have the answers, perhaps no one did and there was to be a long struggle.

One day I surrendered. Finally I could breathe again when internally I took my desperate hands off of handling everything and let God be in charge. I continued to seek all available help, but I no longer felt alone. Not that I didn't stay on top of everything and still long for a solution. I did the foot work and tried to truly let God take charge.

It is with pleasure today that I admit, "I don't know." Because I don't. What a freedom. Giving up playing God to anyone or about anything is not my job, never was.

Today I'm better at not dragging yesterdays behind me. When I remember to do this I stay in the now, as best I can, and what a gift. Everything everywhere is already all right within when I stay in this very moment. Yes, there is power in the simple sentence: I don't know.

"Let's Face the Music and Dance"

Looking at old movies I see Fred Astaire and his dancing partner Ginger Rogers gracefully twirling around the dance floor to the song, *Let's Face the Music and Dance.* The delight in the rhythm of the swing songs continues in widening circles even today.

The song tells us that there may be clouds and rain in life, that there will be dreary days. The song also reminds us we have a choice. We can sit and moan about disappointments and failures, or we can get up and dance.

We would all prefer that the background music of our lives keep producing happy notes and blended sounds that please the ear, but such is not possible.

We can run from the seemingly dry, arid surroundings in which we find ourselves. We can go to greener pastures, seek the beauty of coastal scenes but eventually most of us have to walk through the desert spiritually if not physically, in one way or another.

I always have found great strength and beauty in the desert, both the actual, physical desert and the inner desert that at times I am cast into. In fact, at times the inner desert is precisely where I need to be to learn the lessons that are specifically designed for me, lessons I cannot learn any other way.

Observing the much loved desert of west Texas where I grew up, I see tiny, delicate wild flowers which carpet the ground in colors of purple, orange, and yellow. In the clear air of the desert the sinking sun emphasizes wrinkles on the bald mountains which the wind has carved.

I find serenity and spirituality in the expansive scene of the west, a sense of personal perspective exists in the wide expanse that does not exist anywhere else for me. The quiet, the silence brings me inside where I find truth. Offering my nothingness to God, I find an inner peace that will survive any storm.

When life comes along and delivers blows, we can choose to allow ourselves to be cast into the desert, finding the strength and courage that we had all along. We can turn and run from challenges, or we can simply metaphorically, *Face the Music and Dance* even as we stand still.

Old Games

"Your paper is the last to be taken in!" my neighbor announces to me with glee. Living in a high rise I have two neighbors on my floor. One neighbor's husband loves to see who is the last to get up in the morning and retrieve the paper lying by our doors. I believe he thinks, "Last one's a loser!" My immediate response wants to be an excuse, as if I were embarrassed. But I merely smile.

Some ladies in the building claim the most trips out for the day. "I spent the morning in class, then picking up the grandchildren from school, and then I had to…"

"Well, I went to Pilates and have been on errands all day it seems," the other friend boasts with a smile.

I wish I could be amused by the vying of my own friends to be on the top of my call list.

"Why didn't you call?" Sarah asks me, and Mary replies, "She was having lunch with me."

This old game of competition goes on and on, from the best of the best to the worst of the worst. In families sometimes, if one can't be the best student, most obedient, then that sibling might settle to be the worst. My own brother was ultra-risky. His adventures ranged from sneaking dad's car at night to take his little sister for a ride, to accidentally setting the house on fire by lighting matches and watch them go down the clothes chute in our house. It seemed as if he was most proud in taking the lead at upsetting our parents.

One hears all the time the lament of people trying to have the most serious problems.

Who has the hardest road to walk, who has never had a break?

What a waste of time. People are created as separate individuals, there is no duplicate for who we are. The most necessary truth to face is that life is not fair. It isn't. It is not "tit for tat" either.

It is said that men compete and women compare. If that is so, and it seems to be, that kind of situation only creates division, separation, and the raising up of the twin problems – jealousy and resentment.

Why can't we just…let it be?

Dare to be Vulnerable

What stops me from letting go and exploring life fully, exposing myself to different people and nature's astounding beauty? Poet Mary Oliver in her magnificent poem, *"Have You Ever Tried to Enter the Long, Black Branches?"* says what stops us from opening ourselves to everything are those dark shouters, caution and prudence. Those words so engrained from childhood admonishments linger and grow stronger it seems as the years go by. Roger Housden in his *Ten Poems to Set You Free*, says of Mary Oliver's poem "caution and prudence have their place in life, but we so often heed their calls when we least need them. If we follow their every command, we shall forever be teetering on the edge of life, keeping a safe distance, in imagined control of our experience and environment."

I believe fear closes windows and doors upon unexplored treasures. Never mind the possibilities out there in the world. Things are fine as they are, at least things are familiar the way they are right now. "Don't rock the boat" dominated much of my life. Keep everything nice and smooth. Also, I never trusted my own insights when I was young. Naively I accepted another's statements as being absolute, especially if they were in a position of authority. They must be right.

To continue the poem, Oliver's vision of a sea journey: "A small boat flounders in deep waves, and what's coming next is coming with its own heave and grace." I so love that vision. What a relief it is to finally know that there is so little control I have over much in life. Someone or something larger than I can ever imagine is in perfect control. This belief helps me let go of any fear of each dawning day. I'm only cheating myself if I erect invisible barriers around myself, imagining protection – from what?

Releasing doubts in daily meditation assists me in letting go of imagined control. At least that is the goal. It's one I must renew every day.

Risk

And then the day came when the risk to remain tight in a bud was more painful than the risk it took to blossom.

Anais Nin

If there is one thing I believe about life it is that everything changes, nothing stays the same. If things seem to be great for me at this moment, I can be assured this will not remain the same. It's not that it has to become awful, or difficult. It's just that our thoughts will change, circumstances will evolve into something different – not better, not worse, just different. And if things are difficult, I can hang onto the knowledge that this too will change.

I thought my ideas of people, once formed, would remain the same. I found that a person I believed was honest and good can disappoint me and leave me feeling bereft when that belief was challenged. It's not that suddenly they became evil, it is more that this individual is exhibiting human behavior. I am free to forgive, or hold this person forever responsible.

I believe that I am free to risk changing my understanding of everything; I'm free to modify, to transform ideas, free to finally respect and show loving care to my own person. I am free to choose another road, though it may appear to be impossible at one time, it is never too late to change, to choose another road.

I can look with fresh eyes upon each day, staying right in the now, or I can choose to operate with yesterday's concerns or tomorrow's fears. I can lament the weather turning, the season's relentless progression through the years, or I can lower my expectations upon my mind and body as the years roll by, treasuring what abilities are left.

I believe that there is a power not seen that, if trusted, can assist me through my days. This unseen higher presence can and does direct my actions. The only prerequisites are belief, trust and my request for guidance. I have to ask. I believe this power never fails to provide, although the result may look negative, it is always unbelievably steady and presents a much better outcome than I could have planned myself. Time and again, I sit back, shake my head, smile and marvel at events that are unveiled upon my request for help.

Finally, I believe I am here on earth for a purpose, and it is my firm belief that this purpose will unfold if I remain open to change. Nothing stays the same.

The Way Through

I believe there are two ways to let go of the judging mind. Richard Rohr introduced me to the thought that great love and great suffering are the ways to let go. I believe this because I've experienced this relief for myself.

When I fell deeply in love, everything and everyone was washed in gentle acceptance, the world and I radiated good will. The things that bothered me before, bothered me no more. My generous love seemed to spill onto everything and everyone.

Then the juxtaposition of extreme loss:

The jaws of death were wide and greedy and began with the death of my mother, followed by husband, son and daughter. I would begin to recover my sea legs only to be slammed back onto the hard cement of reality once more.

The other side of the coin: After waves of shocking, unexpected losses, a letter from my cousin, Tom, arrived, containing the words that resonated deep inside. It was exactly what was happening to me.

He said, "You know the difference between pain and agony. Pain is a piece of cake, something you can talk about and leave behind. Agony becomes a part of your future that can't be relayed. It's you now, and you'd never taste the depth of who you are without it. It's a gem you wouldn't ask for, neither would you ask that it be taken away."

The sliver of understanding widened. As with great love, in the core of despair I was shocked to find a sense of quiet, of peace – as if I sank to the bottom of the lake, thereby having a surface from which to push back up, to breathe, to live. I reached out to my faith.

I asked God to grant me his comfort and the courage to go on. Trusting that this would be given, I received that strength and have it until today. I'd been trying to hold myself together, only to discover I was being held all along.

To my surprise beneath the grit of grief I found honey. Even my surroundings took on depth. There was no need for my mind to divide, blame or judge anything anymore. Condemnation faded into the background – of no importance now.

Being human, I at times fall back into the desire to control, fix, explain and have answers, but I can call up the beautiful freedom and try to live within its bounds – just for today. And that is enough.

Strings of the Kite

Admit it. We all like to play God at times. Our minds tell us that it is all up to us, that we can control, change, or rearrange the people and the situations they find themselves in. We see their problem. We can help them change things.

But that's like trying to change the forms in a puzzle we're working or choosing another color for the forest.

Children are the kites we launch in life, expecting the trajectory for them to be straight up and steady, hopefully with no sudden dips or interference. Here we stand with two or more strings in our hands. Yep, it's up to us.

We don't want anyone else to handle our kite. This is ours.

It doesn't occur to us that there are other people who stand by, others who are ready and willing to take the string for a while. Raising a child might look to us as if we're running with the kite, filling it with air. That's our responsibility. We guide our young, but there is a time when we must just let go, transfer the string to other, perhaps stronger hands, release our grip on where we think this kite should go, which direction will be followed.

As Hilary Clinton once said, *It Takes a Village* to raise a child. That should be a relief to most parents but it's not always. Some want the control back. I'm sure upon reaching adulthood most all of us remember one or two teachers, neighbors, friends who supported and gave us priceless gifts towards maturity. Kahlil Gibran says in The Prophet:

> *Your children are not your children.*
>
> *They are the sons and daughters of Life's longing*
>
> *For itself.*
>
> *They come through you but not from you,*
>
> *And though they are with you yet they belong not to you.*
>
> *You may give them your love but not*
>
> *Your thoughts,*
>
> *For they have their own thoughts.*
>
> *You may house their bodies but not*
>
> *Their souls,*
>
> *For their souls dwell in the house of tomorrow,*
>
> *Which you cannot visit, not even in*
>
> *Your dreams.*

Harmony

What comes, let it come.
What stays, let it stay.
What goes, let it go.

Papaji

This saying congers up a feeling of peace within me. It's a lesson I'm open to more and more. Its essence is simple, and one that I am comfortable with. The lesson is to stop fighting anyone and anything. Actually, fighting is something I have deliberately avoided, being conflict phobic (that in itself can become a problem.)

But seriously, what this little poem reveals to me is an understanding which if practiced will lead to surrender and peace. How many of us bristle at the word surrender. I did too for a long time.

But, having been confronted with my own powerlessness over so much of life's happenings, surrender becomes a calming word, not an embarrassing word. It's rather like awakening to discover that I've lifted my lids upon a new way to participate in life.

Hopefully I'm done trying to force life's events into the shapes and forms I picture in my mind – "the way it should be." In a perfect world everything would flow easily. The river's path would be unimpeded. But it doesn't work that way. There are boulders in the river of life, big ones. And at times all we can do is unclench our tight fists and let what is, be.

I don't like change. I want things to stay as they are. When I place my bed on a certain wall – there it stays for as long as I stay. I wanted my children to remain at the gentle, amenable eight and nine years of age. I want my body to perform tasks with ease as always.

The only thing that remains unchanged is the placement of my bed. And that is because it's inanimate and can't walk off.

Only thing I can think of to do with all of this is relax and let go. Try and live in this moment. Be grateful for what simply is this day. I am grateful and hopeful right now. And I'd like to stay this way. I won't, but I'd like to.

Oh So Peaceful

One summer day I was driving by myself to our lake house, my family was to join me the next day, and I found myself absolutely exhilarated by the mere fact of being by myself for one whole day. I was raising four children at the time. This brief time alone was precious to me, time to breathe, to gather my thoughts, to just be in the moment.

As I drove I sang along with the radio. "It's oh, so peaceful here...nobody leaning over my shoulder, nobody breathing in my ear..."

I rounded the bend in the road, opened my window, and bellowed out the song.

How precious I found that time. I sat on the deck of our little lake house and gazed at the sun sinking below the western hills, leaving a trail of bright orange on the horizon. As I dreamed and mused a sense of guilt enveloped me. Here I was enjoying myself while those at home were going about their daily activities. I should be there to make sure the children were getting off to school on time, I should be checking their clothes packed for the lake. But you set all that up before you left, I told my worrying mind. An inner voice intoned, "Yes, but a mother's job is never done. It's yours to do and do properly."

A friend's inquiry just the past week had left me puzzled. "What do *you* need?" she innocently asked. I had no reply, no idea what she meant. No young mother of my acquaintance ever indicated to me that they felt the need for time of their own. Since marriage and parenthood I had not stopped to ask myself such a question. It was irrelevant.

What do I need or want? I didn't have a clue. But I knew that the one thing I used to do and did not have time for anymore was to sit and dream, to muse, and to write. Buried in the back of my closet were journals, stories I used to write, poems that had flowed out of me, essay on happiness, pain, and life. I had put away things of my childhood, folded up my talent between soft layers of memory and stowed those bright tiles away from sight and mind.

I opened drawers in the kitchen and found a grocery notepad. I began with the song I had heard that morning – "nobody leaning over my shoulder, nobody breathing in my ear" and when I finished I had written four pages. With a deep sigh I went to bed, wondering with anticipation what time my family would be here the next day.

GRATITUDE

Book Marks

"What marks your place in the world? What turns you on, fires you up, what are you passionate about?" I teach a creative writing class and I ask my class these questions at the beginning of each semester.

If book marks keep our place in books we read, what keeps our place in the world?

I say too quickly that my heart keeps my place in the scheme of my days. But too often this is a struggle. People intrude, duties assume large importance, and worldly things interfere. For too long, I put people, places, and things ahead of knowing myself. One day I enumerated to a friend the tasks I was involved in to fix things for others and take care of their desires and wants. She gently asked me, "What do you want?" – such a simple question. I paused and thought and finally answered, "I haven't a clue."

Friends and family have an important place in my life and in my heart. But in the midst of being in the busy world, I had no idea where I fit, where I naturally belonged. I didn't know what to look for. I'd marked a place in my book of life for everyone and everything, but when I examined these places, I didn't seem to find me lurking in any corner. In short, I didn't have a clear view of who I was or what I wanted.

Slowly as I turned the pages of my life I found clues here and there. Like a movie run backwards, I saw where I glowed up in the mountains, bloomed in the park and smiled inside and out with a creative writing class. I heard a whoop of joy watching myself with my grandchildren swimming with the dolphins. Most of all I saw myself, as I matured, stepping out of the coloring lines more and more. In fact, I delight in stepping out of the lines others have for my life. Out the window went the guilt of enjoying myself, and I heard a Whoopee! coming from me.

I saw myself finding my own path and having decided which direction to head, I watched a more defined person step forward to lead her own life.

Why did I take so long to mark my place – in my life, in my world? I don't know. Perhaps I was too busy collecting smiles for my behavior and marching to the same beat as others. It's not that I'm now creating off-key tunes that jar; actually it's quite the opposite. My tune is quiet and gentle and guides only me, but it feels real. It feels authentic. I found my place and marked my book of life with my heart.

Our Own Special Ticket

In one of Ann Frank's statements in her moving account of being hidden from the Nazis she said, "He [God] won't give us the ticket until we're on the train." Of course this statement can be interpreted different ways. I believe it means that during extreme duress or stress we are not given a way to cope until we have accepted the situation exactly as it is – we are on the train, it is happening and we are called to respond.

I've found in my own life that it is only at that moment when I've exhausted every way out of pain, that I can step back, surrender, and ask for outside help from a higher source. It seems so simple an act, but total release of any idea that I am in control must be set aside – pushed off the cliff of possibilities, so to speak.

The invisible strong hand of the ego's control is difficult to spot. Most of us go along building our paper identities, which is a necessary process in the first half of life. It's not that we discard this important function. We add to it later in life. Many of us cling to this stage in ignorance of the ego's pervasive pull. I know one of my dad's mantra was "Never give up." How brave I thought, how right that statement is. And sometimes it is the thing to do, no question. But life's experience presented the other side to me also. At times the more I struggled, the more I believed my way was the right way, the more pain my inner being felt. Lonely was that path.

Society encourages going with the status quo. Go along with popular thinking, listen to the voices of reason and logic, which mostly comes from our already formed views. I participated in this for many, many years.

I was carried along the status quo, fitting into the established current of the day. But somehow I felt off center, untrue. We have much to contribute out of our individual experiences and their interpretations as we live it. We need not copy to feel worthy. I feel that my small puzzle piece fits perfectly into a special place in the universe that nobody else can fill.

The Treasure of Surprise and Delight

In his poem titled, *"A Brief for the Defense"* Jack Gilbert presents the thought that joy needs defending. In Roger Housden's book, *"Ten Poems to Change Your Life Again and Again"*, he interprets this poem beautifully. Housden writes that the poor and desperate know better than most that it is how we respond to suffering that makes all the difference. The shared experience of poverty with others in the same circumstance is why they can laugh more heartily than those protected by good fortune. Sometimes those buffers lead the fortunate ones into either denial or guilt. The AA Program is a perfect example of the true connection between the surrendered.

Roger Housden in his wisdom explains that in childhood a lesson that many are taught is that if we raise our voice above the crowd, we lay ourselves open to ridicule, criticism, and envy. And that, he says, can silence us for years, even for a life time. We doubt ourselves, we doubt our own voice, our inspirations, the joy of our own creative urges – all for the sake of keeping the peace and preserving the mediocrity of the social norm.

Wendell Berry says,

Why all the embarrassment
About being happy?

In his poem Jack Gilbert contends, "We must risk delight. Be willing to stand out, be different, to live in full abandon to the life that is rising inside you, no matter what anyone else around you might say."

I well understand this. There have been times when I suppressed creative ideas for fear of being different. My youthful motto was, "don't rock the boat."

After my husband died, I remember the guilt when I let myself feel happy – about anything. Further loss of close family and friends to the jaws of death increased the underlying guilt of letting myself go in laughter, in joy, in pleasure. However, I recognize today that because of my suffering, my laughter comes from the belly, not the vocal cords. And I welcome it.

I see how more intensely I feel life. There is a core in me of solid determination to live my life fully. The pain carved deeper inside the well of who I am, of my spirit. I no longer live nonchalantly. From the depth of sorrow I understand my increased ability to love, to enjoy, to laugh out loud, to make no excuses for just being me in the midst of joy. I treasure these moments and live to share them.

The Bees of Life

Roger Housden, in his book *Ten Poems to Say Goodbye* talks about an image of Antonio Machado:

And the golden bees
were making white combs
and sweet honey
from my old failures.

Housden says, "Imagine the possibility that every single turn of events, however dark or disappointing the outcome, can in some circuitous way be the raw material for something that eventually surfaces with the sweetness of honey. The heart, like the grape, is prone to delivering its harvest in the same moment that it appears to be crushed."

The day I realized that I had lost all, that there was no thing to hold onto was the day I fell headlong into life – as it is. I gave up anxious fighting. I gave up having to have answers. Instead I very slowly stepped forward into life with surprisingly more zest than I thought I possessed. It was as if I watched this woman move through the pain, watched her begin teaching classes, investing energy in things which she previously had little interest.

I've begun to say, "I appreciate you" more often to those I engage with daily. It was Richard Rohr who said, "Instead of saying prayers all day, it's more about being a prayer." It's about showing up. It's about an inner peace that accepts the imperfect not only in others but in oneself. It's about simple gratitude. I'm learning to be thankful for my flaws, because it is through the imperfect that the appreciation of the sweetness of life emerges. The crushed flower emits its fragrance.

Finally I understand when people talk about the blessings that can come from loss.

Trust/Release

Returning from physical therapy, I became aware of a human factor in receiving help. In trying to loosen tight muscles the therapist had to ask me every two minutes, "relax, let me have the limb" when the automatic response is always holding onto. Sure enough when I let go of control the pain decreased.

Trust is the issue. It's a matter of trusting the therapist. How many times we are called upon to trust. Why is it so hard?

I put my money in the bank. I have to trust it will be safe. I pick out a beautiful red tomato in the grocery store. I have to trust that it carries no germs to hurt me. To a woman, her hair is the crowning of her beauty. We have to trust the beauty operator – "Don't cut it too short." "Style it like this picture," we say. We climb in our cars every day and go to work. We have to trust that the car will get us there and we have to trust that the building that houses our work will still be standing.

Every time we get on a plane, we trust that we will arrive at our destination. Some remain fearful on every flight. I am lucky. I love the rush that taking off provides me. It's a matter of trust again. I consciously let go of any control. I say to myself, "It's a go! Give it your all! Go for broke!" As the plane lifts off the ground I close my eyes and smile, feeling in my bones the immense energy that lifts the plane off the ground.

When it comes to people it's another story. A lot depends upon our experiences in our youth. If we were let down, disappointed, downright abused, trust will not come easily. We'll have to learn to practice trust where everything in us denies it even exists. We have to learn to trust our insides when giving this precious commodity, trust, to another human being.

When my gut relaxes, when my eyes are comforted by the sight of another, I slowly recognize that trust is building. It feels good, this trust. It becomes a life line. The person shines a light in the sometimes darkened halls of life. When I recognize it, how welcome that is.

People Illusions

I see the same faces when I go to my Continuing Education classes. At coffee break there is one woman who stares at me across the room a lot, without expression. She just stares. I smile and she looks away.

I feel a chill coming from her, and so I make up a story in my head about her. She's always "turned out in an attractive, scholarly outfit." I'm in jeans. For some unknown reason she doesn't like me. My story about this evolves. She thinks the class I teach is frivolous, and she judges it as being less than the classes she takes, which happen to all be very historically correct and requiring a lot of study. I teach Creative Writing.

A woman in our building seems to avoid talking to me. So, I create another story. She's shut down and somehow I remind her of someone that she has known in her past. This past hasn't been pleasant and I remind her of the unresolved situation.

Living with these assumptions, these stories without checking anything out becomes a sad waste. The story lines, unchallenged, harden with time. One day I decided to dispel these questions by making an effort to know and understand these people. At coffee break at school I walk across the room right to the woman who stares at me. "Hi" I say, "I see you at break and wonder what class you are taking. I'm looking for another class to take."

Lo and behold, she pleasantly answers and we engage in small talk for a while. She becomes less of an enigma and has become a school friend.

Same with the woman in my building. I smile at her, ask her questions about her day, initiate conversation in the hall or in the elevator. I always get a smile back. Such a simple gesture of a smile to others who appear before me each day makes us both feel better.

Assumptions about family members happen all the time. I make up story lines about what is going on or has gone on. I freeze them in a past role and don't let them change or grow. Possibly I carry long held opinions about how I was treated or how I was not treated and these, without resolution, harden through the years.

I become weary of trying to connect with some people yet I hold tight to the box I've put them in, clinging to my made up stories. So, I decide to have a conversation about this, open the doors of this dusty basement, let in some fresh air. It's scary to be real. But win or lose, let the understanding, the unveiling begin! When we open doors together, things change for the better.

Like Dorothy and her friends, I decide to pull back the sheet of "unknowing." And guess what? The feared wizard of Oz, huge in my mind, is exposed – not as some scary, frightening presence who doesn't like me, but as another human being, faults and all, just like me. I can love without fully understanding but understanding gives so much more.

As a Man Thinketh

In the forward to James Allen's book, *As A Man Thinketh*, the author states that he hopes to stimulate men and women to the discovery of the truth that they are makers of themselves by virtue of the thoughts which they choose and encourage; that mind is the master-weaver, both of the inner garment of character and the outer garment of circumstance."

I clearly see the result of my thinking on my actions today. As with most things, the first step to change is the recognition of how we operate. Even more than this, the recognition of the results of our thinking.

Time and again throughout life, new experiences did not meet the thoughts I had about them before the event. I envisioned a coming situation as boring when it turned out to be exciting, or maybe it's the thought that everybody on the other side politically is totally unjust, unkind and just wrong, when political beliefs are never all right or all wrong. The desperate condition of separation and division that exists today reminds me of the growing inability to let another thought different from mine to enter my mind, to allow that alien thought that deserves at least a look-see.

Where the real rub is when we imagine we know what others are doing or thinking and we react according to this unexplored view. I was a master at this guessing game, being afraid to check things out with another. I assumed I already knew. How many times connection goes awry from these thoughts.

I've found that usually I get what I expect. I draw towards myself that which I think about. That's the hidden promise I too often forget.

It seems a key to identifying this problem is to ask a trusted person to give us feedback on what they see in us that is keeping us from our best. It's true that we cannot read ourselves correctly. It's like the blind spot on our back that we cannot see.

So, I guess the lesson, at least to me, is not to lock my thoughts in a self-manufactured "truth box" but understand that if I am open, more will be revealed – always.

Meet Them Where They Are

Sometimes I continue to expect some important people in my life to give back "in kind." I'm thinking, I want the same level of appreciation and love that I give to you. Then the hope goes to, "this time it will be mutual, we'll connect on the level that I'm wishing for."

It's like tasting a pudding that looks like chocolate, but never is. Yet I keep expecting that flavor to be there. Or it appears to be a deep river and I'm excited and prepared. I've got my life belt on, my rowing arm strong, and I'm ready to tackle the job of getting through the rough rapids. Only the river turns out to be shallow. There are no rapids.

To keep expecting and being prepared for what is not coming reminds me of the saying,

"To keep doing the same thing over and over, expecting a different result, is the definition of insanity."

Just meeting people where they are sounds so simple. But resistance seems hard wired in me. Brain ruts are deeply carved. Reactions turn on automatically. My thoughts frequently sabotage the very things I crave.

It might just be that we all have different levels of awareness, different levels of capacity.

I picture two people swimming in a lake. One has problems swimming as well as problems of emotional distress. It's not for me to pull this person along. It's not for me to push from behind. It works best and most comfortably if I just swim along gently beside her.

Surprising Support

I feel I've endured the very worst, I lived the impossible nightmare of every parent – I lost to early deaths two of my children. In the deep darkness an amazing thing can happen – you find yourself opening into what you don't understand but seems to be a gentle power that is lifting you up. After having lost what you thought you had to have to live, there appears a weird sense of calm murmuring deep inside. I was trying to hold myself together when I found that I was already being held.

Several days after I'd experienced this relief I had a vivid dream: I was trapped under water in a frozen lake, there was nothing but a thick sheet of ice above me. I asked myself what am I going to do, and somewhere inside a calmness, an answer came, "We'll just have to learn how to breathe underwater" and then finding that I could do the impossible – in my dream I took a breath under water.

Much later I was stunned to learn that there was a poem one I'd never read or heard about, and a series of tapes about the ocean and breathing underwater. How to explain…

Every day I continued with surrender and prayer in deep gratitude for being found by a love that sustained me, a love that surpassed anything I could even imagined.

I felt as if I was being ever so tenderly carried now through my days. Was this real? Did I dare to trust this? Yes, I did, an underground trust of God facilitated this extraordinary fact. There is a difference between saying "I believe" and knowing the complete trust.

I knew that I wanted with all my heart to reach out to others who have lost children – it seems that there are more parents having this tragic experience than one would think. I found some of these mothers and offered my experience and my hope. We would meet for coffee and talk and talk and talk. We talked until we felt some relief of pain. I had always known the saying that "Sharing pain halves it; sharing joy doubles it." But now I experienced firsthand the truth that by the simple act of vulnerability, of trusting another with my pain I felt less alone, less drained. I finally caught the faint breeze of hope.

Fences

Driving down familiar streets I'm noticing yards and houses these days. The ones with the proverbial white picket fence catch my eye, and I'm thrust into an image from childhood. It's a safe and ever so pleasant view, these homes encircled by a little white fence. Red roses sometimes are planted near-by.

I picture the families living in these homes. It's a fairy tale existence in my mind, where everyone is smiling. There is laughter and joking going on, and life is enjoyed to the hilt.

However pleasing these thoughts, I now believe that these pretty little fences can work in other ways: keeping people out, or keeping people in, separating "us from the others."

The mind loves to judge, classify and measure. But there is another possibility that seeks out the best of both, finding common ground in each.

Some of us erect fences around our hearts following severe loss. I did that myself until I realized that yes, those fences might be limiting my risk for more pain, but they also limited joy. Today I choose to unlock that fence and leave it, if not open at least ajar. I've come to see that there is validity in most situations and points of view. Sometimes I do not know the good news from the bad news.

The pain of circumstances beyond my control have widened me inside, forced me to confront my illusions, the white-fence syndrome. Sometimes this information is more than I'd like to acknowledge.

The spiritual message of all great religions have mainly one message, which is "Wake Up."

If Not You, Then Who?

A little girl walking towards me in the park with her dad and her dog suddenly broke away and skipped right up to me. I stopped and bent down, "Hi. What a nice morning for walking your puppy," I said. Her little hands folded at her chest as she grinned. We chatted for a moment, her dad smiling beside us. "Well, I must be going," I said. Then I noticed her little t-shirt. It said, "IF NOT YOU, THEN WHO?" I looked at the father. Smiling all around, we parted. Small treasured event.

These five words echo within, saying to me this particular day, "If life is going to be better for you and others, what are you willing to do? If not you, then who?"

This child trusted herself to run up to me and stop and I bent to show her she was important. The child's innate trust most of us have had since childhood. I've had correct signals coming from my heart, my feelings, all my life but they've been minimized mainly by society. Intuition, the ability to recognize and use symbols has been slighted for a century; logic, facts took over and we left the soul side of ourselves on the shelf, far, far too long.

Small gifts like this morning happen to me a lot, especially in the park. And I think it's because I'm looking for them, each day I'm open to see them. One might say through losing two of my children to early deaths, I've been cracked open to everything. The worst has happened. I did survive. I know from experience that even events you think will destroy you completely, even those have a gift. Something changes, rearranges, adjusts the soul within. Although you did not think you could survive, you now have a strength you did not have before.

For my birthday a friend, Annie, gave me a tiny angel, her arms raised high above her upturned head. I internalize that pose and especially when things look gloomy, I will lift my arms high, throw my head back to look at the sky, and take a deep breath. Who is going to offer comfort in the world? "If Not You, Then Who?"

Have Answers

Have answers, will travel. Such an enterprise might seem enticing at first glance. Oh, boy, there's some guru who promises to soothe my worried brow, some wise person the hem of whose collegiate gown I can hang onto.

Most of us don't truly trust ourselves. I prefer trusting other people. An extreme example: I was talking with a friend who said, "We missed you at the meeting." I looked puzzled for a moment but said nothing. I left her thinking, "I could have sworn I was there last month, but maybe my memory fails me." Actually, I had been at the meeting, but Helen must know, right? My first instinct is to make others right – to ignore my own consciousness.

In the past I looked outside myself for answers to my problems. I turned to professors, adjusted my diet, got into physical exercise. At times I went around asking peers and those in authority for advice. I read copious quantities of self-help books. I took the presenting puzzle but too often didn't try to fit the pieces together myself.

I did most of these things until I ran out of gurus. There was one advisor, God, I always believed in, but belief and total trust are different things. It wasn't until I ran out of gas, ran out of answers and could go no further that I turned away from the strong but equally disappointing need for some assurance that things would not change, that there was some predictability to life. I was being prepared to let go in a real sense

– let go of the intense urge to get an exact blueprint before me to follow, to know exactly what came next.

I so wanted to be in charge. The pain of loss was the tool that leveled me and took away false pride. Came the day when I asked God for help. Not a fancy, scripted lovely prayer but a simple admission that I needed God. A request as simple as "Help." And then I remained quiet for some time. Silently and softly I felt the release. The continued repetition of surrender slowly revealed a release from the returning inner lists, questions, and statements. A sense of calm and a knowledge that I was where I was supposed to be at this time, and that God was right there with me entered my being. It presented itself with simplicity. It was a quiet and natural shift in perception.

There is less need to have written instructions anymore. I may still desire them but I don't have to have explicit explanations and data corroborating the information anymore. It's okay to rest in the questions, in the mystery.

Enlightenment

The following is informed by a wonderful, world renowned spiritual guide, Father Richard Rohr:

The age of Enlightenment is misnamed. Today we see that this title was precisely not that at all. The Enlightenment era covered three centuries, 17th, 18th and 19th, before consciousness grew and we woke up to the fact that pure knowledge wasn't enough for the second half of life. The so-called Enlightenment wasn't celebrating the whole person, it didn't promote or encourage the wisdom of inner experience. As Father Richard Rohr said, we finally learned very simply that education is not transformation. We ignore the soul at our detriment.

During the Enlightenment era there was the big push to stay in the head, because facts resulted in accomplishments. It was concentrating mainly on logical left brain thinking. There was nothing wrong with that. It is where we all necessarily start life. It just isn't enough. It left out much of the personal, the warmth of the heart, the spiritual self. For centuries children simply were not rewarded for their feelings. They were only applauded for results and awards that one could see.

As in the old T.V. show, "Dragnet," Sergeant Friday insisted he wanted from his subjects "Just the facts, mam, just the facts," when a character was trying to explain their feelings about an event.

This concentration on learning largely ignored the acknowledgement of a spiritual life. Because devotion, especially to something that doesn't produce visual recognition was low priority. No one is to blame, few want to go about unlearning things that didn't work, letting go of people and habits. The work of the spirit entails that process and few people willingly want to do that.

I am blessed to have been aware that life is more than what one can see and touch. I've been blessed to know that there is more, much more, in the unseen of life, beyond the visible. That there are deep wells of wisdom hidden inside.

I might not have fully explored my own soul and inner strength had life not taken away my expected steadiness of continuity: marriage, children and friends. When those major staples began to disappear one by one from my life, I had to explore in depth life from the inside. No books, classes, or maps could accomplish this. It was with my desperate seeking, my need to "lean into the pain"; "ask God for help" that I surfaced. Trusting that I need to ask God for guidance and comfort, I willingly did this. I received it then and to this very day. Every time I ask for guidance and comfort, it comes in many ways, sometimes in a phone call, sometimes in someone appearing who needs my help.

Strangely enough, through deep pain sometimes arrives astounding, hard won wisdom.

Hope

James Finley made a statement in one of his talks that struck a beautiful chord in me.

He said, "Having endured the worst you can sometimes come upon the best of the best." I took that to mean finding the best would not have appeared without having gone through the worst of the worst. That statement expresses perfectly the unexplainable situation in which I found myself after the loss of four major family members, one after the other.

I knew on a deep level that to survive myself somehow I had to find a thread of gold in all of those losses. I had to discover a path out of the extreme pain and I knew I could not do it by myself. So, I read, I prayed, I listened daily to CD's of Richard Rohr and James Finley. I looked for others who were in grief so that we might share our path to recovery together. We would get together, not to just cry and lament. We found humorous events and characteristics of our loved ones over which we could laugh, we remembered treasured occasions.

Slowly, I emerged from the cocoon of grief and sure enough I found a beautiful butterfly emerging. The freedom slowly emerged, freedom to participate to the full in life again.

I dwelled upon a simple statement that a minister in Houston, Texas told me long ago.

He said to the worried mother that I was at that time, "Remember this, everything everywhere is already all right." In other words the situation was necessary for some growth to take place. This short wisdom sentence reminded me of how very little I was in control of much of anything. All I could do was the best that I was capable of at that time. I was to work in tandem with advice from wise friends, spiritual guides and professional help. And above all to keep detached from pushing the river in what might be the wrong direction.

That sentence gave me the open door to hope. Or as the unknown author said, "It will be all right when it's over. If it's not all right, it's not over." Good news.

GRACE

A Big Yes!

I believe the human spirit can heal and be stronger than imagined, especially after one of life's blows. My husband died on the operating table during his third heart operation. He was only 61. We had six and a half years of blissful marriage, for which I remain grateful. However, I remember the shock and devastation I experienced at that time. For months after Don's death I sat in stunned grief until a friend gently asked me, "What is it that you've always wanted to do and have not allowed yourself to do?"

My response came easily, "Learn to fly."

After this conversation, I sat awhile with the enticing thought of flying. I had raised four children, survived a divorce, reconnected three years later with the love of my college life who was a widower, married him and moved from Texas to Colorado. Perseverance showed up at each turn of events.

One day I investigated flying lessons. The next day I followed through, driving to the little Centennial Airport outside of Denver. My instructor was awaiting my arrival. After my lesson, as I walked from the little Cessna to the terminal I smiled as my mind conjured a picture of Amelia Earhart striding away from her little plane, white scarf blowing behind her.

Severe losses were hidden in the future for me. I didn't know that this flying experience would supply some lessons needed to survive the coming deaths of my son and my daughter, to build a store of trust again in the world, my God and in myself. After these tsunamis of severe loss, belief in those imperative things had slowly leaked away like air escaping from the bright balloon of life.

With my instructor's gentle guidance and persistent encouragement I was thrust into another dimension. I learned the necessity of staying totally present in the moment, to sharpen my awareness, to let the instruments guide me, to gain perspective on my petty irritations by looking down upon this beautiful earth from on high.

I learned that I could trust my God to supply the courage and strength to survive anything. If I so chose, I could put aside the wiles of the world. I could finally be safe in the midst of sand storms.

Dream

A dream that lingers in my mind is this one:

I am on a sail boat in the middle of the ocean. My good friend, Joanne, is out with me for a fun day of sailing. For some reason I need to climb up to the top of the sail to adjust something. The wind has picked up. I find I need a tool and call down to Joanne for it.

There is no answer. I call again. Again, no answer. I look down on the boat and there is no one there. I realize with each hefty swell of the ocean that I am very much alone.

This dream occurred at the same time of the end of my first marriage. This upheaval was long in coming and although it turned out to be the only and best thing that could be done at that time, the loneliness for all of us during this time was depicted by my dream.

Sometime later I came across this by Ramakrishna:

The winds of grace
Are blowing all
The time.
You have only to
Raise your sail....

What a lovely thought. It points out the raw fact that there is a power we can tap into, an energy available to all. Life suddenly shook my world in earth quakes of loss and the lack of equilibrium allowed me to find this power from the deepest me.

There was a choice involved. I could either sit in a corner, avoiding what appeared to be approaching pain, or I could turn and face full force what each day presented.

I uncovered an indomitable spirit coupled with a determination to go forward, no matter what. When the worst has happened, there is no more to fear.

Kingdoms

Richard Rohr's thoughts swing wide a lot of doors for many of us, my own Ahh-Haa's come fast with his words.

This one is especially revealing: We all know the prayer phrase, "Thy Kingdom come." Richard Rohr calls to mind the necessity to also consider, "My kingdoms go."

I believe most of us aren't aware of the tiny kingdoms, the absolutes that we create in our lives. They can be anything we worship, consciously or unconsciously. Let's see if I can think of some.

When young, our parents are the kingdom. All knowing, sometimes wise guides, sometimes not, they certainly can be buffers against the loose world. Dependable or not, they truly are the only kingdom children know. And amazingly, for some, their influence, good or bad, even reaches beyond the grave.

In our teen years most of us had our peers as a kingdom. What they thought, what they wore, how they behaved was paramount in our thinking. They became our guides. Now I see why who my friends were was so important to my parents. I watched some friends at school get caught up with the wrong crowd and disappear from their healthy lives.

Young adulthood presents its own kingdoms: mates and babies become our island.

We place careers high up in a kingdom all its own. All this is rightly so. But along with heavy responsibility comes the temptation to ease the stress and some fall into coping habits that takes a toll.

Excessive eating, drinking, pill taking, shopping, on and on goes the list of addictions. Some people recover from this, many do not.

As the years go by, other kingdoms appear. The pitfalls of the three Ps – power, possessions, and prestige – loom large on the horizon. The natural push towards recognition in life can spill over into the temptation to worship the dollar. And the sight of our names in lights can beckon like a strong magnet.

I believe most of us have many false kingdoms that develop through the years. And it isn't until the second half of life that the opportunity to re-evaluate comes. Something was lacking for me when I tried to live this second half of life with the same game plan as the first. Things that worked before no longer served me.

After the deaths of four major immediate family members I was surrendered. The slate was wiped clean. I no longer had answers. I had to learn to live with the questions. I couldn't do that with just my head which demanded explanations. I fell deep down into my spirit. I had always believed in God, but now I found in the depth of despair, a new trust in God. When all else failed, my faith and trust, aided by my direct asking for help from above, gave me the new game plan. Promoted by complete surrender, I feel a wholeness never before experienced. For that I am grateful.

Stretcher from Heaven

For most of my life I believed that knowledge was all I needed. Higher education staunchly indoctrinated that life would be much better if academically prepared and that is true.

While knowledge has its place, it was life that led me to uncover and value what lies deeper, beyond the words of scholars. Beneath pure information lies a deep well of pivotal resources that I did not tap until forced to do so through adversity. The beginning of a favorite poem of mine by Rumi, "Zero Circle," states:

Be helpless, dumbfounded,
Unable to say yes or no.
Then a stretcher will come from grace
To gather us up.

Rumi goes on to say:
We are too dull-eyed to see that beauty
If we say we can, we're lying.
If we say No, we don't see it,
That No will behead us
And shut tight our window onto spirit.

I believe the author is telling me that to truly find God and discover His grace, I have to be rendered helpless, dumbfounded. The

Twelve-Step programs know this. In fact, they offer that only in a state of surrender can we be rescued, freed from the bondage of addiction. No moral psychology or adherence to rules ever kept an addict from his bedevilments. Rumi ends his poem with this:

> *So, let us rather not be sure of anything*
> *Besides ourselves, and only that, so*
> *Miraculous beings come running to help,*
> *Crazed, lying in a zero circle, mute,*
> *We shall be saying finally,*
> *With tremendous eloquence, Lead us.*
> *When we have totally surrendered to that beauty,*
> *We shall be a mighty kindness.*

No matter how strictly I follow the rules, keep up the appearance of worthiness, follow society's dictates of the right marriage, the right house, the right job, often I can't find that worthiness until I fail. When the academic lessons ring hollow, the rules suddenly seem empty. Finally I find that worthiness is not found on the outside, in the world that measures and judges. It seems that only in my despairing moments can I admit that by myself alone I cannot find peace, within or without.

Once I can say without reservations, "I don't have the answers," that dependence on formal education alone has failed me in finding inner peace, then and only then am I "gathered up by a stretcher from grace." Magically, I am propelled into willingness to ask for help from a power greater than myself. That acceptance brings relief and comes as knowledge that no matter how grim the circumstances that surrounds me, deep down all is well. I cannot know future outcomes and that fact is okay. There is guidance above and beyond my small egotistic mind. I welcome that gift with all my heart and pray to continue to nurture it.

To Suffer or Not

Take the same set of circumstances with the possibility of hurt feelings and give it to two different people. One might take offense immediately, the other only laugh. One might voice displeasure by aiming a retort back, while the other person may ask for clarification.

I believe the response depends upon the inner climate of each person. Everyone at times has periods when their self-esteem dips below the acceptable line. Few are those of us those who can consistently deal positively with perceived or real rejection or blame.

I find myself less and less sensitive to other's comments on the whole. Finally I have learned that when a misunderstanding takes place and I feel threatened, the part of me that takes offense is usually my ego. I find that the misunderstanding between me and another might be caused by the fact that my friend is having a bad day, his or her comments may be revealing an inner conflict that is permeating their thoughts and has little to do with me and our relationship.

I can take an off the cuff comment and make it into an arrow aimed at my heart. If I want to I can personalize anything and everything. All I am aware of these days is a decision about whether to go to the effort of suffering over this, or not. It's my choice.

I think of the ocean and the beach. Each tiny grain of sand contributes its share of bulk to make a beautiful scene. Transforming that to the human condition, I am only one of those tiny grains. I need not take myself so seriously.

Meditation

The only person not present in the room that I can talk to out loud, without disdain from others, is God. That being said I confess that I, living alone, frequently have conversations with myself – yes, out loud. Even in the grocery store, albeit said quietly under my breath, "Should we have chicken again?" "Which brand of Kleenex?" "Shall we buy flowers for ourselves?" (That answer is always yes!)

Strangely, I rarely speak to God out loud. I whisper prayers, eyes closed. It amuses me to find how often when praying for others that I diagnosis the problem, and then go right ahead and prescribe the solution for God to perform. What arrogance.

For some time now I find my daily balance by the habit of morning meditation. It isn't talking, it isn't begging, it isn't anything more than sitting still and letting go of the whistle stops my brain makes every few seconds. Father Keating teaches the way to be uninvolved with the minutiae is to acknowledge the thoughts, place them on a boat and send it down the river. "Okay, there's another thought – I put you on the yellow boat, go." At times when someone whose presence is very annoying comes to mind, I confess I put that one on a dark purple boat and send it down the river fast.

This simple practice is like the popular sit-com "Seinfeld." It's about nothing. This fact befuddles a lot of people. We are a society of accomplishments, of action, of assignments to categories. I picture that mind-set as a line of pigeon holes, where everything is neat and tidy. That's fine as far as it goes. But that line doesn't breathe.

I believe my practice of letting go of my thoughts permits a rise of consciousness to a new level.

Would that this knowledge will keep me going, allowing me to live more readily in the now.

I Know Nothing of Tomorrow

"I know nothing of tomorrow except the love of God will rise before the sun" That is the beginning of a song my daughter, Jeanine, sang in the Memorial Drive Presbyterian Church children's choir.

I'm just now fully acknowledging the need to truly let go of the useless expectations that crowd into my mind each day. It's just now that in many ways I feel like I'm "hitting my full stride" in life. I feel that everything that's happened before has led up to this very minute when I can harvest that for which I have labored so hard. And that is freedom. The freedom of exemption from having to live a life that was "thought best for me" by others, freedom from fitting in the conventional wisdom of the times, from thinking it is I who can change any loved one's beliefs or behaviors. The freedom to be true to myself is an enormous joy.

I have survived much loss in life. Today it's hard to imagine what could possibly destroy my hard-won equanimity. Surprisingly, I can now honestly say that those losses that burrowed so deep in my heart, also contained a jewel. That was a gentle peace that I never would have attained without these tests. I was taught by them that there is a source of strength, courage and hope that I by myself could never have managed. This strength is invisible to the eye. Only when I could say out loud, "I don't know" and "I need help" did this energy swoop down and cover me with an amazing release. I call this presence, God.

I've also discovered a delightful "child" inside me that I've kept throughout everything. She is letting herself indulge in playfulness to the hilt. I let her roam wherever she wants providing it's safe for her and others. She has led me into unimaginable joy. She lets her natural affection shower upon people she likes, and calls to their minds that we are mirrors to each other – what we spot in another is a part of ourselves or we couldn't see it in another.

This playful inner child makes a daily game of looking for the good in people, of smiling at others, offering a spot in traffic, simple gestures of good will. Life is so harsh, everyone is carrying a burden. I consciously try and add a small amount of sunshine. It seems to be true: Whatever we give, we get back.

I believe that the good thoughts we encourage in ourselves can spill over into a bit of joy in the lives of many, like the taste of hot chocolate on a cold winter's day.

Liquid Oxygen

When I was growing up, my father had a good friend whose business was liquid oxygen and he had a big plant on the west side of El Paso. The only thing I learned about this substance was from listening to an explanation my brother received when he made a visit to this plant. Dad's friend showed him how you could freeze a flexible rubber tube by dipping it in liquid nitrogen. It would then break like glass if you snapped it in two or crushed it underfoot.

I remember this in later years when I think about the universal need for forgiveness. If I dip my mistakes or those of others into the hardness of liquid nitrogen, my unforgiveness, I can easily be broken, crushed in the pool of shame and blame. The pliable tube of experience hardened by the unforgiveness of others and of ourselves, can break the spirit to where it will never again be flexible.

Judgment abounds when we are growing up. We are measured and weighed against others. The internal measurement of ourselves can be the most severe. We weigh ourselves and inevitably find ourselves lacking in one area or another. It is only when we accept and forgive ourselves that we can fully extend that gift to another. So much of my life growing up was lived in the division of people into good or bad, better or worse, on top or on bottom of the totem pole. How limiting the illusion of division was.

Where do we find forgiveness? If not in ourselves, if not in authority figures, then where? I grew up with a firm belief in God. But in later years I did not find an abundance of the quality of forgiveness in the traditional source, the church, so much as in a community of people who were admittedly flawed. It was in the company of others who were leveled by their own faults, who came to accept themselves and others unconditionally that I found true love and forgiveness. It was in rooms of humble acceptance of our human condition where competition was finally eliminated and I joined the human race. It was here that I learned that forgiveness of others began with forgiveness of self.

It was with seeking souls that I found my belief in God firming into trust. Human understanding through history has at times depicted God as a judging, punishing deity who did not really like us very much. How could I trust a vengeful higher being? Just as I cannot go to a superior, righteous person in trust, I had to take the mask of a punishing God off and found that His love and forgiveness was there in abundance all along. And I found Him in the everyday, the simple, the mundane. Examples leapt out of the ordinariness of people, of life. I look daily for the simple offering of God's supportive, loving presence.... I find it because I am looking for it.

Who You Is and Who You Ain't

Most of us grew up and still believe that we are our thoughts. What we think is who we are. Since we were taught to give total control to the mind, of course we thought we were that person who mostly used logic to formulate our lives.

Wishing Will Make It So was my mother's favorite song. I think she honestly thought that was true. And she passed day dreaming on to her daughter, me. While I day dream still, I am aware it is only a dream, while I think my mother on some level bought into the naïve illusion that somehow "wishing will make it so."

A personal practice of contemplation has opened doors for me that are astounding. Never would I have imagined that simply sitting quietly for 20 minutes, eyes closed, each morning could bring such inner peace. I do this by not fighting the useless thoughts that pound through my human mind. Giving all thoughts the same value, no big deals, I sometimes achieve release from the battering of ideas that clamor for my attention. Though I fail in this effort every day, still I know it is the goal. Another tool I use against idle thoughts is to picture a puppy I am trying to train. The puppy wanders off the paper. With no judgment I reach out and gently bring the puppy back, time and again.

The bonus is a new awareness of who I am. Although I still have my judge's robes on about people and events, I am now conscious of the waste this practice presents. Most people are doing the best that they know how. I am positive that our Maker made originals, none better or worse than another on the inside. Some are misled, some are their own worst enemy, but they came into the world as an individual.

Who I ain't is that person who strove so hard to "fit in," the person who denied her own belief system to incorporate that of another just to please that person.

Someone said, "I'm not who I was; I'm not who I'm going to be; but I'm on my way." I am more authentic as I grow in awareness of my true self.

Up Close and Personal

I've always had a faith in God. At times others have asked for me to explain that faith.

It's so elusive. It's so personal. It floats just out of sight of explanation. It's a mystery. Most of us don't like mysteries, except those we read in a book that solve an incident.

Still I strive to paint mental pictures of this astounding phenomenon so important in my life, to voice this with clarity to anyone should they ask. I can't.

All I know is that this powerful invisible source can and is most willing to be with me, to guide me and to comfort me. This doesn't happen at the snap of a finger. It's a repetition of belief, trust and a quiet place to be. And it seems I have to ask for guidance. For most of my life I would "think" how nice it would be if God would help me out here. Or wouldn't it be great if God could solve this huge problem. It didn't occur to me to ask for this help. I thought, I wished, I wanted, but I didn't ask. One thing I did realize early on, my God is not a bell boy to grant silly requests for monetary things.

Along came the deaths of four immediate family members, one right after the other. Picture the air-filled clown balloon at a child's birthday party. You can stand before it and punch it hard. It bends backwards and touches the ground. But it bounces back. That's apparently what I did, come back each time. But it wasn't easy, it wasn't instant, it wasn't without a whole lot of tears and prayers.

I attended my church's grief group, consulted with a therapist, doctors, ministers and read copious books on loss. I added others who suffered severe losses to my contact list.

We would get together and share over coffee, supporting each other with our stories.

And yes, we found laughter again. Lots of fond memories of those passed on. We pictured them laughing with us. We were sure they were present at our meetings.

With each demise of a treasured, loved one, I surrendered deeper to God. One particular night at an all-time low, my body, my mind, and my spirit sank to my knees and I cried out to God, "I can't do this anymore. Please take this agony..." Staying still, eyes closed, after a while I felt a calmness fall over me, a quiet, gentle wrapping around of my body ensued. I slept the night in total peace that had not occurred before that very night. This presence has stayed by my side and has given me strength, courage, and life. I could not do life without it.

So that is the best I can do to describe the wonderful miracle of compassion and love that I received, unearned, with immense gratitude. All I had to do was accept what was always offered.

Night Pages

This world is far more generous, more beautiful and breath-taking than human beings can contemplate. At times I can feel the underpinning of something so grand, so stunning that it seems too big for universal awareness. It's beyond comprehension.

This awareness is fleeting, but I sense in my very being that there exists something so mighty, so powerful and magnificent that I can only stand in awe. It's like there is a tiny rip in the fabric of common reality and I get to see another reality for a moment in time.

I can't name it but I feel its vibes humming, now strong, now weak, but always present. This energy cannot be described in words. It seems that there is a giant rhythm that exists in the world that once I tap into it, I am connected and when I choose to recognize this, it feels like underlying hands girding my very existence.

I believe that there is something in the universe accompanying me that can only be experienced. It cannot be explained by logic, by pure intellect, cannot be found in a text. No words are adequate to explain this phenomenon. It exists for all, only most remain unaware of its existence and potential, until great need or a crisis appears on the horizon.

I believe that my thoughts result in actions that in turn define my life. And if I can let go of my need to control, this energy will assist me in my choices. The thoughts that dominate my thinking are like magnets, attracting those very things into my life. If I let go and deeply believe that a strong force is guiding me along my path and am open to this, circumstances occur which are far better than anything I, by myself, could have arranged.

Some of my belief systems were installed in the early years. I absorbed attitudes and stances from the environment without apparent choice. These silent directives switch on early in life and some of those reactions can last a life time. I'm grateful for the pain that woke me up.

A key for me is staying connected. Remaining separate only increases my isolation from reality and the deep river of wellbeing. For me, human contacts together with that unseen, precious force, is paramount to maintaining a strong vine of life. I deeply believe that the truth is the truth wherever it is found and that there are many paths that lead to God. And I believe that all beings are born loved, accepted and forgiven by God.

I've heard this from Richard Rohr: "There is a necessary light that is only available in darkness – in suffering – that you cannot know any other way." I found that true for me.

This presence was and remains so strong that any doubts I have about being alone in the world are swept away. What magnificence!

About the Author

Patricia Forbes was born and raised in El Paso, Texas. Her family moved to Houston where she married and bore four children. Patricia attended Mr. Vernon College in Washington, D.C. and the University of Texas. She received a Bachelor of Science degree in Education. In later years she moved back to her beloved mountains and now resides in Denver, Colorado.

She wrote and published numerous articles and stories in journals and magazines. One of her articles appeared as the feature story in *NAMI Advocate, The National Voice on Mental Illness* in 2002.

For 14 years Patricia has been a regular memoir writing facilitator for Osher Lifelong Learning Institute (OLLI), through the University of Denver where she also taught classes about the second half of life. She attributes her inspiration for her writing life to the vision of the Rocky Mountains as seen from the window of her home near Washington Park.